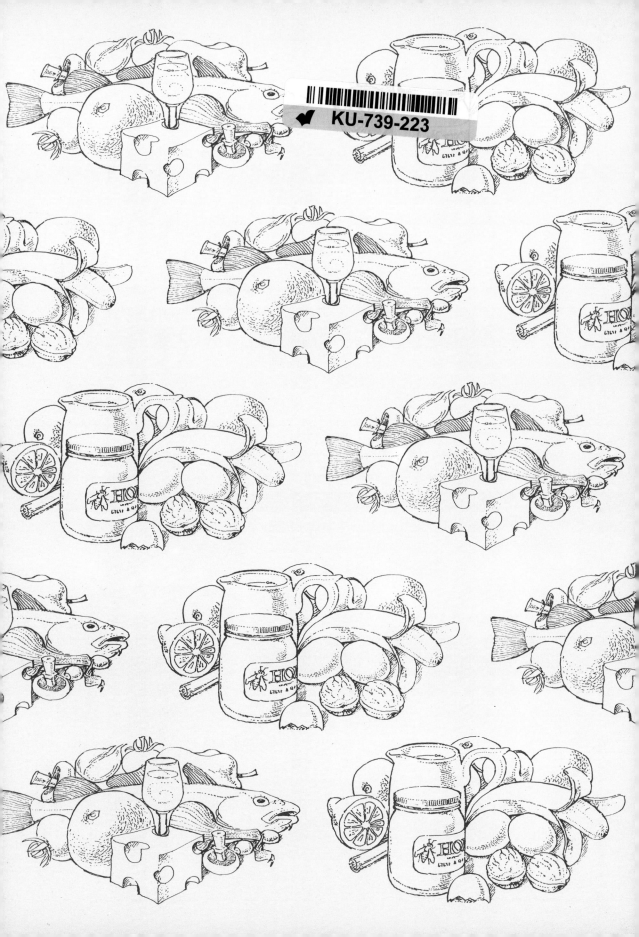

Kellogg's
COOKBOOK

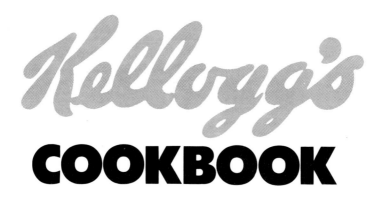

COOKBOOK

Over 130 tested recipes for all occasions

HAMLYN

London · New York · Sydney · Toronto

Published by
The Hamlyn Publishing Group Limited
London · New York · Sydney · Toronto
Astronaut House, Feltham, Middlesex, England

© 1980 Kellogg Company

Compiled by Victoria Lloyd Davies with the help of five home economists from the
Kellogg's Kitchen – Valerie, Wendy, Jane, Barbara and Eve.

Photography by John Lee and Roy Rich
Jacket photography by Paul Williams
Line drawings by Gay John Galsworthy

ISBN 0 600 35351 6

Filmset by Tradespools Ltd, Frome, Somerset
Printed and bound in Spain
by Graficromo, S. A. – Córdoba

Contents

Useful Facts and Figures

Notes on metrication

In this book quantities are given in metric and Imperial measures. Exact conversion from Imperial to metric measures does not usually give very convenient working quantities and so the metric measures have normally been rounded off into units of 25 grams. This method of conversion gives good results in nearly all cases, although in certain recipes a more accurate conversion is necessary to produce a balanced recipe. The table below shows the recommended equivalents.

Ounces	Approx g to nearest whole figure	Recommended conversion to nearest unit of 25
1	28	25
2	57	50
3	85	75
4	113	100
5	142	150
6	170	175
7	198	200
8	227	225
9	255	250
10	283	275
11	312	300
12	340	350
13	368	375
14	396	400
15	425	425
16 (1 lb)	454	450
17	482	475
18	510	500
19	539	550
20 (1¼ lb)	567	575

Note When converting quantities over 20 oz first add the appropriate figures in the centre column, then adjust to the nearest unit of 25. As a general guide, 1 kg (1000 g) equals 2.2 lb or about 2 lb 3 oz.

Liquid measures The millilitre has been used in this book and the following table gives a few examples.

Imperial	Approx ml to nearest whole figure	Recommended ml
¼ pint	142	150 ml
½ pint	283	300 ml
¾ pint	425	450 ml
1 pint	567	600 ml
1½ pints	851	900 ml
1¾ pints	992	1000 ml (1 litre)

In certain recipes a slightly different conversion has been necessary to produce a balanced recipe.

Spoon measures All spoon measures given in this book are level unless otherwise stated.

Can sizes At present, cans are marked with the exact (usually to the nearest whole number) metric equivalent of the Imperial weight of the contents, so we have followed this practice when giving can sizes.

Oven temperatures
The table below gives recommended equivalents.

	°C	°F	Gas Mark
Very cool	110	225	¼
	120	250	½
Cool	140	275	1
	150	300	2
Moderate	160	325	3
	180	350	4
Moderately hot	190	375	5
	200	400	6
Hot	220	425	7
	230	450	8
Very hot	240	475	9

Kellogg's Energy Chart

Products	Energy per 100g	
	Kilojoules	Kilocalories
Maize:		
Kellogg's Corn Flakes	1500	358
Frosties	1480	354
Rice:		
Rice Krispies	1470	352
Ricicles	1490	355
Coco Krispies	1500	359
Puffa Puffa Rice	1730	413
Wheat:		
All-Bran	1090	261
Bran Buds	1150	274
30% Bran Flakes	1310	314
Sultana Bran	1330	317
Sugar Smacks	1540	369
Composite Cereals:		
Special K	1510	360
Country Store	1470	361
Cracklin' Bran	1620	387
Extra	1360	325
Miscellaneous:		
Boil-in-the-bag Rice	1370	327

Kellogg's Corn Flakes

Typical Nutritional Composition per 100 grammes

Energy	358 kcal
	1500 kJ
Protein	8.0 g
Vitamins:	
Niacin	16.0 mg
Vitamin B_6	1.8 mg
Riboflavin (B_2)	1.5 mg
Thiamin (B_1)	1.0 mg
Vitamin D	2.8 μg
Iron	6.7 mg

A typical serving of *Kellogg's Corn Flakes* is 30 g. This will provide at least one-quarter of the average adult's or one-third of a child's recommended daily intake of these vitamins, and one-sixth of their iron needs.

Introduction

Ever since they were first introduced 70 years ago, *Kellogg's Corn Flakes* have remained the most popular breakfast cereal in the world. And during that time their value, not only as a nutritious ready-to-eat breakfast food, but as a convenient and versatile cooking ingredient, has been recognised by cooks everywhere. Most cooks will also know that this versatility applies to every cereal in the now extensive range of *Kellogg's* maize, rice, wheat and bran-based products.

This cookery book is a collection of recipes devised and tested over the years by *Kellogg's* home economists, featuring not only the cereal products, but other foods made by *Kellogg's* too. It brings together a wide choice of recipes for soups and starters, main meals, vegetable and salad dishes, desserts, baking, children's recipes, drinks – and, of course, breakfast. It contains ideas for every cooking requirement – from everyday family meals to party entertaining. A convenient guide for the complete needs of today's cook, *Kellogg's Cookbook* aims to offer *the best to you*, not only each morning but throughout the day.

THE CEREAL STORY

Maize, wheat, rice and oats and their nutritive value have been the staples of man's diet since the beginning of civilisation. The processing of these cereals into ready-to-eat form was one of the great innovations in food technology which have helped to change the dietary habits of people throughout the world.

Nutritious Food

Corn Flakes were the first ready-to-eat breakfast cereal. They were produced in the early 1900's in the small town of Battle Creek, Michigan, where Dr John Harvey Kellogg had his sanatorium. He first made *Corn Flakes* as a nutritious dietetic food for his patients, and his brother, William Keith Kellogg, the business manager of the sanatorium, soon realised the commercial potential of the invention.

Expansion

After 18 years of remarkable success in America, during which time *Kellogg's* developed *All-Bran* and *Rice Krispies*, the Company was encouraged to introduce all three products to Britain by 1924.

The introduction of cereals to the British market was to bring about a radical change in British breakfast habits, and *Kellogg's* now produce over a million and a half packets of cereal a day, for UK consumption alone.

Added Benefits

Cereals can increase the nutritional value of recipes as they are a good source of vitamins and minerals. *Kellogg's Corn Flakes*, for example, are fortified with five different vitamins and iron, and also add wholesome flavour and a rich appetising colour to many dishes.

Dietary Fibre

Whole grain cereal is also an important source of dietary fibre, or roughage, needed to allow the digestive system to function efficiently. And bran, consisting of the outer layers of wheat grains, is the most common form of cereal fibre. Bran-based cereals like *All-Bran* and *Bran Buds* are rich in fibre and, whether eaten on their own with milk or used in cooking, are invaluable in ensuring that the family has a healthy diet.

Economical Extenders

Another benefit of cereals is that they can all be used to make main meals go further. A meat loaf using 675 g (1½ lb) freshly minced beef will take 75 g (3 oz) bran cereal, improving the flavour and making the loaf go further.

Cereal Cookery – First Steps

You can use cereals for crispy toppings, crunchy coatings or economical extenders – all of which will make many recipes more tasty and nutritious. But before you begin, the following general directions will help ensure that your cereal cookery is a success.

There's a simple way to crush *Corn Flakes* and that's to put the *Corn Flakes* into a polythene bag, seal and crush with a rolling pin.

There are two methods of using bran cereal in cooking. The first is to soak it in milk until completely soft, and then to add it to the creamed mixture. Alternatively, it can be added to the recipe along with the meat or dry ingredients.

Breakfasts

Breakfast often follows a fast of up to twelve hours – the longest in the twenty-four hour cycle – and literally means 'breaking the fast'. Nutritionists agree that breakfast should give us one-quarter of the day's protein and energy requirements, and supply vital nourishment to replenish the body when its blood sugar level – which affects both physical and mental energy – is at its lowest. A cereal breakfast supplies the body with protein and energy and also fibre, another important part of the diet. Fibre, also known as roughage, provides bulk in the intestines and is needed to allow the digestive system to function efficiently. Other important nutrients which should be included in a healthy diet are vitamins and minerals – such as iron, found in cereal products, and Vitamin C, plentiful in fruit drinks.
It is always important to eat a good breakfast and make a bright and healthy start to each new day.

The Kellogg's Breakfast

Illustrated opposite

1 portion *Kellogg's Corn Flakes* (approx. 30 g) with milk (125 ml) and sugar to taste

juice of 1 orange or 1 glass fresh orange juice (125 ml)

2 slices wholemeal brown toast (50 g) with butter and marmalade to taste

1 glass milk (150 ml)

This breakfast will give you:

Calories	6.34	Iron	3.8mg	Vitamin B	0.7mg
Protein	16.4g	Vitamin A	300.0μg	Niacin	3.0mg
Carbohydrates	85.8g	Thiamin (B$_1$)	0.5mg	Vitamin C	37.5mg
Dietary Fibre	7.5g	Riboflavin (B$_2$)	1.4mg	Vitamin D	1.0μg
Calcium	350.0mg				

*The **Kellogg's breakfast** (see above), Dark orange marmalade (see page 20).*

Dark Orange
Marmalade

Fruit and Nut Bowl

Serves 4

Metric		Imperial
350 ml	**natural yogurt**	12 fl oz
25–50 g	**hazelnuts, finely chopped or crushed**	1–2 oz
2.5 ml	**ground cinnamon**	$\frac{1}{2}$ teaspoon
2	**bananas, sliced**	2
2	**oranges, segmented**	2
	Kellogg's Sultana Bran	

Mix the yogurt, hazelnuts and cinnamon together. Stir in the bananas and orange segments, divide between four cereal bowls and sprinkle *Sultana Bran* over the top of each.

Kipperee

Serves 4

Metric		Imperial
100 g (1 bag)	**Kellogg's Boil-in-the-bag Rice**	4 oz (1 bag)
1 (170-g) packet	**frozen kipper fillets**	1 (6-oz) packet
15 ml	**chopped parsley**	1 tablespoon
2	**eggs, hard-boiled and chopped**	2
15 ml	**tomato purée**	1 tablespoon
	lemon wedges to garnish	

Cook the rice according to packet instructions. Drain well. Cook the kipper fillets according to packet instructions then flake with a fork. Mix all the ingredients together in a bowl, cover and leave overnight in the refrigerator, if liked. The following morning, turn the mixture into a frying pan and reheat slowly, turning occasionally. Serve on a heated dish, garnished with lemon wedges.

Egg and Bacon Breakfast Burgers

Serves 4

Metric		Imperial
1 (127-g) packet	**instant mashed potato (5–6 servings)**	1 (4½-oz) packet
	a little beaten egg	
15 g	**butter or margarine**	½ oz
2	**eggs, hard-boiled and chopped**	2
4	**rashers back bacon, fried and chopped**	4
	salt and pepper	
	Worcestershire sauce (optional)	
	Coating	
	beaten egg	
	***Kellogg's Corn Flakes*, finely crushed**	
	oil to fry	

Make up the potato as directed on the packet. Add a little beaten egg and the butter and mix well. Cool then stir in the hard-boiled egg, bacon, seasoning and Worcestershire sauce. Shape the mixture into eight cakes. Dip each cake into the beaten egg and coat with the crushed *Corn Flakes*. Lightly fry the burgers in oil, turning once, until golden brown on the outside and heated through.

If liked, the burgers may be prepared and coated then left covered in the refrigerator overnight, ready to cook for breakfast.

Crunchy Mushroom Pot

Illustrated opposite
Serves 4–6

Metric		Imperial
25 g	**butter**	1 oz
1	**onion, chopped**	1
175 g	**button mushrooms, sliced**	6 oz
40 g	**plain flour**	$1\frac{1}{2}$ oz
200 ml	**stock**	$\frac{1}{3}$ pint
200 ml	**milk, including top of the milk**	$\frac{1}{3}$ pint
	salt and pepper	
15 ml	**chopped parsley**	1 tablespoon
	Topping	
15 g	***Kellogg's Corn Flakes***	$\frac{1}{2}$ oz
25 g	**Cheddar cheese, grated**	1 oz

Melt the butter and lightly fry the onion and mushrooms (reserving three slices for garnish). Stir in the flour and cook for a minute. Remove from the heat, pour in the stock and milk and bring to the boil, stirring. Season to taste, add the parsley and pour the mixture into a flameproof dish. Mix together the *Corn Flakes* and cheese and sprinkle over the top. Garnish with the reserved mushrooms and place under a preheated grill until the cheese begins to melt.

Brown-Eyed Susans

Serves 4

Metric		Imperial
	Kellogg's Country Store	
	milk	
1 (213-g) can	**prunes, drained**	1 ($7\frac{1}{2}$-oz) can
1 (312-g) can	**mandarin oranges, drained**	1 (11-oz) can

Sprinkle *Country Store* into four cereal bowls and pour over a little milk. Put three prunes in the middle of each bowl on top of the cereal and arrange mandarin oranges around the prunes to make a flower pattern.

Golden brunch bread (see page 16), Crunchy mushroom pot (see above).

Golden Brunch Bread

Illustrated on page 15
Makes 1 loaf

Metric		Imperial
50 g	**Kellogg's All-Bran or Bran Buds**	2 oz
150 ml	**milk**	$\frac{1}{4}$ pint
100 g	**butter, softened**	4 oz
100 g	**soft brown sugar**	4 oz
2	**eggs, lightly beaten**	2
100 g	**self-raising flour**	4 oz
100 g	**dried apricots, soaked overnight and chopped**	4 oz
50 g	**shelled walnuts, chopped**	2 oz

Put the *All-Bran* into a bowl with the milk and leave until the milk is absorbed. Cream the butter and sugar together. Gradually beat in the eggs. Fold in the flour and stir in the apricots and walnuts with the *All-Bran* mixture. Turn into a greased and base-lined 0.5-kg/1-lb loaf tin and bake in a moderate oven (180°C, 350°F, Gas Mark 4) for 1–1$\frac{1}{4}$ hours. Turn out and serve warm or cold, sliced with butter. (The bread keeps moist for up to 10 days if wrapped in foil.)

Honey and Banana Breakfast Drink

Serves 2–4

Metric		Imperial
2	**bananas**	2
1 packet	**Kellogg's Rise & Shine Orange**	1 packet
10 ml	**honey**	2 teaspoons
2.5 ml	**ground cinnamon**	$\frac{1}{2}$ teaspoon
568 ml	**cold milk**	1 pint

Mash the bananas in a bowl. Add the *Rise & Shine*, honey and cinnamon, and gradually whisk in the milk. Pour into individual glasses to serve.

Jack Horner Bowls

Illustrated on page 19
Serves 4

Metric		Imperial
1 (411-g) can	**peach slices, drained**	1 (14½-oz) can
	Kellogg's Corn Flakes	
45 ml	**demerara sugar**	3 tablespoons
30 ml	**desiccated coconut**	2 tablespoons
	milk	
	halved glacé cherries (optional)	

Arrange the peach slices over the base of four cereal bowls and cover with *Corn Flakes*. Mix the sugar with the coconut and sprinkle over the *Corn Flakes*. Pour a little milk over each and serve topped with glacé cherries, if liked.

Canned cherries or prunes may be used instead of peaches.

Lemon Muffins

Illustrated on page 19
Makes 15

Metric		Imperial
50 g	***Kellogg's All-Bran* or *Bran Buds***	2 oz
150 ml	**milk**	¼ pint
50 g	**butter, softened**	2 oz
50 g	**castor sugar**	2 oz
1	**egg, beaten**	1
25 g	**shelled walnuts, chopped**	1 oz
45 ml	**lemon curd**	3 tablespoons
100 g	**plain flour**	4 oz
15 ml	**baking powder**	1 tablespoon

Put the *All-Bran* into a bowl with the milk and leave until softened. Add the butter, sugar, egg, walnuts and lemon curd, and beat well until thoroughly blended. Sift the flour with the baking powder and gently fold in. Turn the mixture into 15 greased deep bun tins or foil cases and bake in a moderately hot oven (200°C, 400°F, Gas Mark 6) for 20–25 minutes, until golden brown and springy to the touch. Serve warm with butter.

Bran, Corn and Sausage Bake

Illustrated opposite
Serves 4

Metric		Imperial
225 g	**sausages**	8 oz
25 g	**lard**	1 oz
25 g	***Kellogg's All-Bran* or *Bran Buds***	1 oz
150 ml	**milk**	$\frac{1}{4}$ pint
40 g	**self-raising flour**	$1\frac{1}{2}$ oz
pinch	**salt**	pinch
1	**egg, beaten**	1
15 ml	**tomato chutney**	1 tablespoon
1 (198-g) can	**sweetcorn**	1 (7-oz) can
	tomato ketchup	

Brown the sausages in 15 g/$\frac{1}{2}$ oz lard and drain well. Place the *All-Bran* in a bowl with half the milk and leave until the milk is absorbed. Sift the flour and salt into a bowl. Gradually beat in the egg and remaining milk. Stir in the chutney, sweetcorn and liquid, and the *All-Bran*.

Melt the remaining lard and pour into a foil pie dish. Arrange the sausages in the dish and pour over the sweetcorn batter. Bake in a hot oven (220°C, 425°F, Gas Mark 7) for about 20 minutes. Serve hot with tomato ketchup.

Breakfast Nog

Illustrated opposite
Serves 2

Metric		Imperial
1 packet	***Kellogg's Rise & Shine* Orange**	1 packet
600 ml	**water**	1 pint
2	**eggs, beaten**	2

Make up the *Rise & Shine* with the water. Heat until almost boiling then quickly pour on to the beaten eggs, whisking. Serve immediately.

Bran, corn and sausage bake (see above), Lemon muffins (see page 17), Breakfast nog (see above), Jack Horner bowl (see page 17).

Three Fruit Marmalade

Makes about 2.25 kg/5 lb

Metric		Imperial
1	**sweet orange**	1
2	**lemons**	2
1	**grapefruit**	1
2 packets	*Kellogg's Rise & Shine* **Lemon**	2 packets
1.4 litres	**water**	$2\frac{1}{2}$ pints
1.35 kg	**granulated or preserving sugar**	3 lb

Scrub the fruit, squeeze out the juice and pips and cut the whole peel into thin strips. Put the peel and juice into a large pan. Whisk the *Rise & Shine* with the water and pour into the pan. Tie the pips in a muslin bag and add to the fruit. Cook gently for about $1\frac{1}{2}$ hours, until the peel is soft. Remove the pips and stir in the sugar until dissolved. Boil rapidly to setting point, when a small amount of marmalade, placed on a cool plate, wrinkles when pushed with the finger. Remove the scum and cool for 30 minutes. Pour into sterilised jars, seal and label.

Dark Orange Marmalade

Illustrated on page 11
Makes about 2.25 kg/5 lb

Metric		Imperial
675 g	**Seville oranges**	$1\frac{1}{2}$ lb
1	**lemon**	1
2 packets	*Kellogg's Rise & Shine* **Orange**	2 packets
1.75 litres	**water**	3 pints
1.35 kg	**granulated or preserving sugar**	3 lb
15 ml	**black treacle**	1 tablespoon

Scrub the fruit, halve, squeeze out the juice and pips then cut the peel into thin strips. Put the peel and juice into a large pan. Whisk the *Rise & Shine* with the water and pour into the pan. Tie the pips in a muslin bag and add to the fruit. Cook gently for about $1\frac{1}{2}$ hours, until the peel is soft. Remove the pips and stir in the sugar and treacle until dissolved. Boil rapidly until setting point is reached (see above). Continue as above.

Economy Marmalade

Makes about 1.25 kg/2½ lb

Metric		Imperial
450 g	**grapefruit and/or orange peel**	1 lb
	peel and juice of 1 lemon	
750 ml	**water**	1¼ pints
675 g	**granulated or preserving sugar**	1½ lb
1 packet	***Kellogg's Rise & Shine* Grapefruit or Orange**	1 packet

Peel the fruit thinly and save the skin in the refrigerator or freezer until you have 450 g/1 lb. Wash the peel and mince together with the lemon peel. Place in a saucepan with 600 ml/1 pint water and the lemon juice. Simmer gently for about 1 hour, until the peel is soft. Stir in the sugar. Blend the *Rise & Shine* with the remaining 150 ml/¼ pint water. Stir into the pan and continue stirring until the sugar has dissolved, then boil rapidly until a small amount, placed on a cool plate, wrinkles when pushed with the finger. Remove the scum and allow to cool for 30 minutes. Pour into sterilised jars, seal and label.

Note This marmalade is made from the skin of ordinary oranges and/or grapefruit which would otherwise be thrown away. It is quite satisfactory to make the marmalade with half the quantity of peel if you do not eat many grapefruit or oranges; use the same quantity of the remaining ingredients to give a less chunky marmalade.

Country Fruit Compote

Illustrated opposite
Serves 4

Metric		Imperial
450 g	**stewed fruit, e.g. plums, apples**	1 lb
50 g	**butter**	2 oz
50 g	**soft brown sugar**	2 oz
100 g	***Kellogg's Country Store***	4 oz

Put the hot stewed fruit into a flameproof dish. Melt the butter with the sugar in a saucepan and stir in the *Country Store*. Spread this mixture over the fruit and place under a preheated grill for a few minutes until golden brown. Serve hot.

Baked French Toast

Serves 4–6

Metric		Imperial
6 slices	**day-old bread**	6 slices
2	**eggs**	2
150 ml	**milk**	$\frac{1}{4}$ pint
1.25 ml	**vanilla essence**	$\frac{1}{4}$ teaspoon
100 g	***Kellogg's Corn Flakes*, finely crushed**	4 oz
50 g	**butter or margarine, melted**	2 oz

Cut each slice of bread into two triangles. In a shallow dish beat the eggs lightly, then stir in the milk and vanilla essence. Put the crushed *Corn Flakes* on a large plate. Dip each bread triangle in the egg mixture, turning once and allowing the bread to absorb the liquid, then coat with crushed *Corn Flakes*. Place in a single layer on a well greased baking tray and trickle melted butter evenly over the bread. Bake in a hot oven (230°C, 450°F, Gas Mark 8) for about 10 minutes, until lightly browned. Serve with marmalade, jam or honey.

Sunday brunch (see page 24), Country fruit compote (see above), Hot brunch drink (see page 24).

Sunday Brunch

Illustrated on page 23
Serves 4–6

Metric		Imperial
75 g	**butter**	3 oz
1	**onion, chopped**	1
3	**lambs' kidneys, sliced**	3
100 g	**button mushrooms, sliced**	4 oz
40 g	**plain flour**	1½ oz
450 ml	**stock**	¾ pint
	salt and pepper	
3	**slices bread, cut into triangles**	3
25 g	*Kellogg's Special K*	1 oz
	Garnish	
1	**egg, hard-boiled and sliced**	1
2	**parsley sprigs**	2

Melt 25 g/1 oz butter and lightly fry the onion, kidneys and mushrooms. Stir in the flour and cook for a minute. Remove from the heat and gradually stir in the stock. Return to the heat and bring to the boil, stirring. Season to taste, turn on to a serving dish and keep warm.

Melt the remaining butter in a frying pan and fry the bread triangles. Place around the kidneys and sprinkle *Special K* over the top. Garnish with sliced hard-boiled egg and parsley.

Hot Brunch Drink

Illustrated on page 23
Serves 4

Metric		Imperial
1 packet	*Kellogg's Rise & Shine* **Orange**	1 packet
2	**bananas, peeled**	2
1	**pear, peeled and core removed**	1
10 ml	**honey**	2 teaspoons

Make up the *Rise & Shine* using hot water. Put all the ingredients into a blender and blend for 12 minutes. Serve warm.

Fruit Compote

Illustrated on page 27

Serves 2

Metric		Imperial
50 g	**dried prunes**	2 oz
100 g	**dried apricots, peaches and apples**	4 oz
300 ml	***Kellogg's Rise & Shine* Grapefruit (made up)**	½ pint
25 g	**low-calorie spread**	1 oz
50 g	***Kellogg's Country Store***	2 oz

Put the prunes with the mixed apricots, peaches and apples into a bowl. Add the *Rise & Shine*, cover and leave to stand overnight.

Transfer the fruit to a saucepan, adding a little water if the mixture seems too dry. Bring to the boil, cover and simmer gently for 15–20 minutes, until tender. Turn into a flameproof dish. Gently melt the low-calorie spread in a saucepan and stir in the *Country Store*. Sprinkle over the fruit and place under a preheated grill until golden brown.

Cheesy Cod Crisp

Serves 1

Metric		Imperial
1	**frozen cod steak, thawed**	1
10 ml	**milk**	2 teaspoons
5 ml	**lemon juice**	1 teaspoon
pinch	**cayenne pepper**	pinch
pinch	**salt**	pinch
50 g	**cottage cheese, sieved**	2 oz
1 slice	**starch-reduced bread, toasted**	1 slice
15 ml	***Kellogg's Special K***	1 tablespoon

Place the cod, milk, lemon juice, cayenne and salt in a pan and cook over a low heat for about 5 minutes. Stir in the cottage cheese and cook for a further 5 minutes. Serve on the hot toast and sprinkle *Special K* over the top.

Crunchy Baked Eggs

Illustrated opposite

Serves 4

Metric		Imperial
15 g	**low-calorie spread**	$\frac{1}{2}$ oz
100 g	**mushrooms, sliced**	4 oz
175 g	**tomatoes, skinned and chopped**	6 oz
	salt and pepper	
4	**eggs**	4
	Topping	
20 g	***Kellogg's Special K***	$\frac{3}{4}$ oz
25 g	**Cheddar cheese, finely grated**	1 oz
15 ml	**chopped parsley**	1 tablespoon

Gently melt the low-calorie spread in a small saucepan. Add the mushrooms and tomatoes and cook gently, covered, for 5 minutes. Season with salt and pepper and turn into a shallow ovenproof dish. Break the eggs into the dish on top of the vegetables and bake in a moderately hot oven (190°C, 375°F, Gas Mark 5) for 10 minutes.

Meanwhile, mix together the topping ingredients. Sprinkle over the eggs and return to the oven for a further 5–10 minutes, until the cheese has melted and the topping is golden brown.

Crunchy baked eggs (see above), Fruit compote (see page 25).

Soups and Starters

A tempting starter to any meal can trigger off the taste buds and create interest for the courses to follow – especially if the starter is one of the delicious recipes prepared for this cookbook.
Hot soups with wholesome bran make warming starters for the clever hostess to include in her menu on a cold winter's evening, while Spiced Nuts and Party Cheese Slices are tasty appetisers – ideal to serve before a cool summer salad. The perfect starter should never completely satisfy the hunger, but merely stimulate the appetite and prepare it for the more substantial main course. From the wide range of recipes included in this section it is easy to choose one which will complement the most basic or exotic dinner menu.

Spiced Nuts

Illustrated on page 31

Metric		Imperial
50 g	**Kellogg's Special K**	2 oz
50 g	**Kellogg's 30% Bran Flakes**	2 oz
100 g	**mixed salted nuts**	4 oz
$\frac{1}{2}$ (100-g) packet	**Pretzel sticks, halved**	$\frac{1}{2}$ ($3\frac{1}{2}$-oz) packet
1.25 ml	**garlic salt**	$\frac{1}{4}$ teaspoon
10 ml	**paprika pepper**	2 teaspoons
pinch	**pepper**	pinch
50 g	**butter, melted**	2 oz

Mix all the ingredients together in a roasting tin. Bake in a moderate oven (180°C, 350°F, Gas Mark 4) for 15 minutes.
   Eat while still warm or cool and store in an airtight container.

Goulash Soup

Illustrated on page 31
Serves 6–8

Metric		Imperial
25 g	**butter**	1 oz
1	**large onion, chopped**	1
1	**large clove garlic, crushed**	1
225 g	**freshly minced beef**	8 oz
1.75 litres	**tomato juice**	3 pints
2	**beef stock cubes, crumbled**	2
5 ml	**salt**	1 teaspoon
2.5 ml	**paprika pepper**	$\frac{1}{2}$ teaspoon
pinch	**pepper**	pinch
100 g (1 bag)	***Kellogg's Boil-in-the-bag Rice***	4 oz (1 bag)

Melt the butter in a large saucepan and cook the onion with the garlic until soft but not browned. Stir in the meat and cook until browned. Add all the remaining ingredients except the rice. Bring to the boil, cover and simmer gently for 15 minutes. Meanwhile cook the rice according to packet instructions. When cooked, stir into the soup and serve.

Cucumber and Lemon Soup

Illustrated opposite
Serves 4

Metric		Imperial
1	**small onion, chopped**	1
450 g	**cucumber, peeled and chopped**	1 lb
600 ml	**chicken stock, made from 2 cubes**	1 pint
150 ml	***Kellogg's Rise & Shine* Lemon (made up)**	$\frac{1}{4}$ pint
15 ml	**cornflour**	1 tablespoon
45 ml	**single cream**	3 tablespoons
	salt and pepper	
	cucumber slices to garnish	

Put the onion, cucumber, stock and *Rise & Shine* into a saucepan. Cover, bring to the boil and simmer for about 20 minutes, until the cucumber and onion are tender. Sieve or liquidise the soup and return to the pan. Blend the cornflour with a little cold water and stir into the soup. Return to the heat, bring to the boil, stirring, and cook for a minute. Finally stir in the cream and season to taste. Serve hot or chilled, garnished with cucumber slices.

Spiced nuts (see page 28), Goulash soup (see page 29), Cucumber and lemon soup (see above).

Smoked Fish Flan

Serves 6

Metric		Imperial
25 g	***Kellogg's 30% Bran Flakes*, finely crushed**	1 oz
150 g	**plain flour**	5 oz
40 g	**butter or margarine**	1½ oz
40 g	**lard**	1½ oz
	water to mix	
	Filling	
225 g	**smoked whiting or cod**	8 oz
1 (150-g) carton	**natural yogurt**	1 (5.3-oz) carton
60 ml	**milk**	4 tablespoons
1 (113-g) carton	**cottage cheese**	1 (4-oz) carton
2	**eggs, beaten**	2
15 ml	**chopped parsley**	1 tablespoon
5 ml	**finely grated lemon rind**	1 teaspoon
	salt and pepper	

Mix the *30% Bran Flakes* with the flour. Rub in the butter and lard until the mixture resembles fine crumbs and add enough water to mix to a firm dough. Roll out the pastry to line a 20-cm/8-inch flan ring or dish and chill while preparing the filling.

Poach the fish in a little water for about 10 minutes, then drain and flake. Mix together the remaining ingredients. Arrange the fish in the base of the flan case and pour the egg mixture over. Bake in a moderately hot oven (190°C, 375°F, Gas Mark 5) for 35–45 minutes, until the filling has set. Serve warm or cold, cut into slices, and accompany with a mixed salad.

Prawn Ring

Illustrated on page 35
Serves 6–8

Metric		Imperial
225 g (2 bags)	***Kellogg's Boil-in-the-bag Rice***	8 oz (2 bags)
100 g	**frozen peas**	4 oz
175 g	**frozen sweetcorn**	6 oz
	Sauce	
40 g	**butter**	$1\frac{1}{2}$ oz
40 g	**plain flour**	$1\frac{1}{2}$ oz
568 ml	**milk**	1 pint
	salt and pepper	
225 g	**peeled prawns**	8 oz
30 ml	**tomato purée**	2 tablespoons
5 ml	**lemon juice**	1 teaspoon
	butter	
	Garnish	
3	**lemon slices**	3
6	**whole prawns**	6

Cook the rice according to packet instructions. Cook the peas and sweetcorn in boiling water for 5 minutes and drain well.

Meanwhile, make the sauce. Melt the butter in a saucepan, stir in the flour and cook for a minute. Remove from the heat and gradually add the milk, stirring constantly. Return to the heat and bring to the boil, stirring until smooth and thickened. Add the seasoning, prawns, tomato purée and lemon juice, and simmer gently for 2–3 minutes.

Mix together the cooked rice, peas and sweetcorn. Butter a 1.5-litre/$2\frac{1}{2}$-pint ring mould and pack the rice firmly into it. Allow the rice to settle, then unmould the ring carefully on to a heated serving plate. Fill the centre with the prawn sauce and serve any extra separately. Garnish with halved lemon slices and whole prawns.

Avocado, Prawn and Fruit Cocktail

Illustrated opposite
Serves 6

Metric		Imperial
300 ml	***Kellogg's Rise & Shine* Grapefruit (made up)**	$\frac{1}{2}$ pint
15 ml	**powdered gelatine**	1 tablespoon
30 ml	**mayonnaise**	2 tablespoons
1	**large orange**	1
1	**large avocado pear**	1
175 g	**peeled prawns**	6 oz
	shredded lettuce to serve	
	paprika pepper to garnish	

Put 45 ml/3 tablespoons of the *Rise & Shine* into a small bowl. Sprinkle over the gelatine and stand the bowl in a pan of hot water, stirring until the gelatine has dissolved. Remove from the heat and stir in the remaining *Rise & Shine*. Put the mayonnaise in another bowl and very gradually stir in the *Rise & Shine* mixture. Leave to set in a cool place, then turn on to a chopping board and, using a sharp, wetted knife, chop the jellied mixture into small cubes.

Cut the peel and pith away from the orange, divide into segments and chop. Peel the avocado and dice the flesh. Add to the jellied grapefruit mixture with the prawns and orange, and mix well together.

Place a little lettuce in the base of six individual glasses or dishes and pile the prawn cocktail on top. Sprinkle with a little paprika just before serving.

Prawn ring (see page 33), Avocado, prawn and fruit cocktail (see above).

Party Cheese Slices

Serves 8

Metric		Imperial
175 g	**plain flour**	6 oz
125 g	**butter**	4 oz
50 g	**Gruyère cheese, finely grated**	2 oz
25 g	***Kellogg's All-Bran* or *Bran Buds***	1 oz
	water to mix	
	Filling	
225 g	**cream cheese**	8 oz
50 g	**blue cheese**	2 oz
15 ml	**creamed horseradish**	1 tablespoon
10	**pimiento-stuffed olives, sliced**	10

Sift the flour into a mixing bowl. Rub in the butter until the mixture resembles fine crumbs. Stir in the Gruyère and *All-Bran* and add enough water to mix to a firm dough. Divide in half and roll one half into a 23-cm/9-inch circle. Place on a baking tray, crimp the edge and prick with a fork. Bake in a hot oven (220°C, 425°F, Gas Mark 7) for 15 minutes. Roll the remaining dough into an 18-cm/7-inch circle and place on a baking tray. Score into eight sections, cutting only part way through the pastry, then cut around the rim of each section to form a scalloped edge. Prick with a fork and bake in the oven for 15 minutes. Cool both pastry rounds.

Put the cream cheese into a bowl. Add the blue cheese and horseradish and beat until smooth. Stir in the olives. Spread this cheese mixture evenly over the larger pastry circle and place the scalloped circle on top. To serve, cut into wedges.

Note For a cocktail snack cut into 16 wedges.

Oriental Cheese Dip

Serves 8–10

Metric		Imperial
1 (113-g) carton	**cottage cheese**	1 (4-oz) carton
225 g	**cream cheese**	8 oz
30 ml	**chopped mango chutney**	2 tablespoons
15 ml	**finely chopped onion**	1 tablespoon
5 ml	**lemon juice**	1 teaspoon
2.5 ml	**salt**	$\frac{1}{2}$ teaspoon
2.5 ml	**curry powder**	$\frac{1}{2}$ teaspoon
25 g	***Kellogg's All-Bran* or *Bran Buds***	1 oz

Put the cottage cheese into a sieve over a bowl and allow the excess liquid to drain away. Mix the cottage cheese and cream cheese together until smooth, then stir in the chutney, onion, lemon juice, salt and curry powder. Chill until the mixture is firm enough to handle, then shape into a ball and roll in the *All-Bran*. Chill for at least 1 hour and serve with savoury biscuits.

Baked Grapefruit

Illustrated on page 39
Serves 6

Metric		Imperial
3	**medium grapefruit, halved**	3
45–60 ml	**sweet sherry**	3–4 tablespoons
50 g	**butter or margarine**	2 oz
50 g	**light soft brown sugar**	2 oz
25 g	***Kellogg's Special K***	1 oz
3	**glacé cherries, halved**	3

Using a sharp knife, cut around the grapefruit segments to loosen, and remove the pithy core from the centre of each half. Spoon a little sherry into the centre of the grapefruit and place the halves, cut side up, in a shallow baking tin. Put the butter and sugar into a small pan and heat gently until melted. Remove from the heat, add the *Special K* and mix lightly together. Spoon over the grapefruit. Bake in a moderately hot oven (200°C, 400°F, Gas Mark 6) for 7–10 minutes and top with a halved cherry.

Celery and Ham Rolls

Illustrated opposite
Serves 4

Metric		Imperial
4	**large sticks celery, halved**	4
10 ml	**French mustard**	2 teaspoons
4	**slices ham**	4
	Sauce	
25 g	**butter or margarine**	1 oz
25 g	**plain flour**	1 oz
300 ml	**milk**	$\frac{1}{2}$ pint
50 g	**Cheddar cheese, grated**	2 oz
	salt and pepper	
	Topping	
25 g	**butter or margarine, melted**	1 oz
25 g	***Kellogg's 30% Bran Flakes***	1 oz
15 ml	**finely chopped parsley**	1 tablespoon

Cook the celery in boiling salted water for about 30 minutes, until tender. Drain well. Spread the mustard over the ham. Put two pieces of celery on each slice of ham and roll the ham up to enclose the mustard and celery. Place in four individual flameproof dishes, or a 1-litre/1½-pint flameproof dish, and keep warm.

Melt the butter in a saucepan, add the flour and cook for a minute, stirring. Remove from the heat and gradually stir in the milk. Return to the heat, bring to the boil, stirring, and cook for a minute until thickened. Remove from the heat, add the cheese and seasoning and stir until the cheese has melted. Pour over the celery and ham rolls and keep warm.

Mix together the butter, *30% Bran Flakes* and parsley and sprinkle over the sauce. Place under a preheated grill for a few minutes, until the topping is crisp. Serve at once.

Baked grapefruit (see page 37), Celery and ham rolls (see above).

Country Chicken Liver Pâté

Serves 6–8

Metric		Imperial
1	**bay leaf**	1
100 g	**streaky bacon rashers**	4 oz
1	**clove garlic, crushed**	1
175 g	**pork sausagemeat**	6 oz
225 g	**chicken livers**	8 oz
1	**egg**	1
60 ml	**milk**	4 tablespoons
25 g	***Kellogg's All-Bran* or *Bran Buds***	1 oz
1.25 ml	**dried thyme**	$\frac{1}{4}$ teaspoon
	salt and pepper	

Place the bay leaf over the base of a 0.5-kg/1-lb loaf tin. Remove the rind from the bacon and, using the back of a knife, stretch the rashers to twice their original length. Line the sides and base of the tin with the bacon rashers.

Mix the garlic and sausagemeat together. Trim the chicken livers and either liquidise in a blender or food processor, or chop them finely. Add to the sausagemeat and mix well. Beat the egg and milk together, add the *All-Bran* and allow to stand for a few minutes, until the *All-Bran* is softened. Stir into the chicken liver mixture with the thyme and seasoning and combine thoroughly.

Turn the pâté into the prepared loaf tin. Cover the tin tightly with foil, stand in an ovenproof dish and pour water into the dish to come halfway up the sides of the tin. Bake in a moderately hot oven (200°C, 400°F, Gas Mark 6) for 40–50 minutes, or until the pâté has started to shrink from the sides of the tin. Leave in the tin until cold. If the pâté has risen above the top of the tin, put a plate and weight on top to press it down. When cold, turn the pâté on to a plate and serve cut into slices, accompanied with hot toast.

To freeze, cool the pâté quickly then turn out and wrap tightly in foil. Freeze quickly. To serve, thaw the pâté, still wrapped, in the refrigerator overnight. Alternatively, the pâté may be sliced before freezing and the slices wrapped individually. Thaw these for about 1–2 hours at room temperature.

Savoury Baked Eggs

Serves 4

Metric		Imperial
15 g	**butter or margarine**	$\frac{1}{2}$ oz
4	**eggs**	4
	salt and pepper	
60 ml	**double cream**	4 tablespoons
	Topping	
50 g	**streaky bacon, chopped**	2 oz
25 g	**Cheddar cheese, finely grated**	1 oz
25 g	***Kellogg's Special K***	1 oz

Lightly butter four individual ovenproof dishes and break an egg into each. Season. Pour the cream over each and bake at 180°C, 350°F, Gas Mark 4 for 5–8 minutes, until almost set. Fry the bacon until crisp then drain and mix with the cheese and *Special K*. Spoon over the eggs and return to the oven for 5 minutes.

Stuffed Mushrooms

Serves 8

Metric		Imperial
16	**large open mushrooms**	16
150 g	**butter**	5 oz
$\frac{1}{2}$	**green pepper, finely chopped**	$\frac{1}{2}$
1	**onion, finely chopped**	1
1	**clove garlic, crushed**	1
generous pinch	**turmeric powder**	generous pinch
1.25 ml	**dried thyme**	$\frac{1}{4}$ teaspoon
	salt and pepper	
50 g	***Kellogg's Special K*, lightly crushed**	2 oz

Wash the mushrooms then finely chop the stalks. Melt 25 g/1 oz butter and fry the stalks with the pepper, onion and garlic. Stir in the turmeric, thyme, seasoning and *Special K*. Add 50 g/2 oz butter and mix well. Divide the mixture between the mushroom caps and press down. Melt the remaining butter in a roasting tin in a moderate oven (180°C, 350°F, Gas Mark 4). Add the mushrooms and cook for 15 minutes.

Main Meals

All the recipes in this section have been compiled to help the busy
housewife create tempting nutritious dishes both for the family and
for entertaining friends. By incorporating cereal products with fresh
foods, it is easy to convert otherwise dull meals into varied and
exciting dishes – while still leaving time to relax and enjoy the meal.
Main meals should be varied, interesting and above all satisfying.
But they should also fit the occasion. Serve hot, filling meals in the
winter and lighter dishes, or crisp refreshing salads, during summer.

Baked Seafood Salad

Illustrated opposite
Serves 6

Metric		Imperial
225 g	**crabmeat, fresh or canned**	8 oz
100 g	**peeled shrimps, fresh or canned**	4 oz
1	**small green pepper, chopped**	1
1	**small onion, finely chopped**	1
3	**sticks celery, thinly sliced**	3
200 ml	**mayonnaise**	$\frac{1}{3}$ pint
5 ml	**Worcestershire sauce**	1 teaspoon
2.5 ml	**salt**	$\frac{1}{2}$ teaspoon
	Topping	
40 g	***Kellogg's Corn Flakes*, lightly crushed**	$1\frac{1}{2}$ oz
25 g	**butter or margarine, melted**	1 oz

If using canned fish, drain. Combine the ingredients and divide between
six deep scallop shells. Mix the *Corn Flakes* with the butter and spoon
over. Bake in a moderate oven (180°C, 350°F, Gas Mark 4) for 20–30
minutes.

*Baked seafood salad (see above), Cheesy potluck casserole (see page 45), Corn-
crisped salmon croquettes (see page 44).*

Corn-Crisped Salmon Croquettes

Illustrated on page 43
Serves 5–6

Metric		Imperial
100 g	**Kellogg's Corn Flakes, finely crushed**	4 oz
1 (170-g) can	**evaporated milk**	1 (6-oz) can
1 (454-g) can	**salmon, drained, boned and flaked**	1 (1-lb) can
30 ml	**tomato chutney**	2 tablespoons
$\frac{1}{2}$	**small onion, finely chopped**	$\frac{1}{2}$
1	**large stick celery, finely chopped**	1
25 g	**butter or margarine, melted**	1 oz
	Sauce	
25 g	**butter or margarine**	1 oz
25 g	**plain flour**	1 oz
300 ml	**milk**	$\frac{1}{2}$ pint
50 g	**cooked vegetables (peas, carrots etc)**	2 oz
30 ml	**double cream (optional)**	2 tablespoons
	salt and pepper	

In a mixing bowl, combine together half the crushed *Corn Flakes*, 150 ml/$\frac{1}{4}$ pint of the evaporated milk, the salmon, chutney, onion and celery. Divide the mixture into 10 or 12 portions and shape into cones or balls. Dip in the remaining evaporated milk then coat with the remaining crushed *Corn Flakes*. Place on a baking tray and spoon a little melted butter over each. Bake in a moderate oven (180°C, 350°F, Gas Mark 4) for about 30 minutes, until golden brown.

To make the sauce, melt the butter in a small saucepan, add the flour and cook for a minute, stirring. Remove from the heat and gradually stir in the milk. Return to the heat, bring to the boil, stirring constantly, and cook for a minute. Add the vegetables, cream and seasoning to taste. Heat through but do not boil. Serve poured over the salmon croquettes.

Cheesy Potluck Casserole

Illustrated on page 43

Serves 4–6

Metric		Imperial
100 g (1 bag)	***Kellogg's Boil-in-the-bag Rice***	4 oz (1 bag)
40 g	**butter or margarine**	$1\frac{1}{2}$ oz
40 g	**plain flour**	$1\frac{1}{2}$ oz
450 ml	**milk**	$\frac{3}{4}$ pint
200 g	**Cheddar cheese, grated**	7 oz
45 ml	**finely chopped parsley**	3 tablespoons
1 (198-g) can	**tuna, drained and flaked**	1 (7-oz) can
	salt and pepper	
	Topping	
25 g	**butter or margarine, melted**	1 oz
2.5 ml	**paprika pepper**	$\frac{1}{2}$ teaspoon
40 g	***Kellogg's Rice Krispies***	$1\frac{1}{2}$ oz
40 g	**Cheddar cheese, sliced**	$1\frac{1}{2}$ oz
	parsley sprigs to garnish	

Cook the rice according to packet instructions and drain well. Melt the butter, add the flour and cook for a minute, stirring. Remove from the heat and gradually stir in the milk. Return to the heat, bring to the boil, stirring constantly, and cook for a minute. Remove from the heat, add the cheese and stir until melted. Mix in the rice, parsley, tuna and seasoning, and combine well. Turn into a greased 1.75-litre/3-pint ovenproof dish.

For the topping, mix together the butter, paprika and *Rice Krispies*, and spoon evenly over the tuna mixture. Arrange the sliced cheese on top and bake in a moderate oven (180°C, 350°F, Gas Mark 4) for about 20 minutes, until heated through. Garnish with parsley to serve.

Crunchy Baked Chicken

Illustrated opposite
Serves 4

Metric		Imperial
4	**chicken portions or drumsticks**	4
1	**egg, beaten**	1
15 ml	**milk**	1 tablespoon
50 g	***Kellogg's Corn Flakes*, finely crushed**	2 oz
1.25 ml	**pepper**	$\frac{1}{4}$ teaspoon
15 g	**Parmesan cheese, grated**	$\frac{1}{2}$ oz
25 g	**butter or margarine, melted**	1 oz

Wash the chicken portions and pat dry. In a shallow dish, mix the egg with the milk. In a second dish, mix together the crushed *Corn Flakes*, pepper and Parmesan. Dip the chicken portions in egg then coat evenly with the crumb mixture. Place in a greased roasting tin and spoon a little melted butter over each. Bake in a moderate oven (180°C, 350°F, Gas Mark 4) for about 45 minutes, until tender. Serve on a bed of watercress leaves and tomato lilies.

Chinese style noodles (see page 48), Crunchy baked chicken (see above).

Chinese Style Noodles

Illustrated on page 47
Serves 2

Metric		Imperial
1 (100-g) packet	***Kellogg's Super Noodles* Chicken Flavour**	1 (3½-oz) packet
30 ml	**oil**	2 tablespoons
3	**large spring onions, chopped**	3
25 g	**flaked almonds**	1 oz
100 g	**cooked chicken, diced**	4 oz
1	**carrot, coarsely grated**	1
25 g	**button mushrooms, sliced**	1 oz
	salt and pepper	
few drops	**soy sauce**	few drops
2	**spring onions to garnish**	2

Make up the noodles according to packet instructions. Meanwhile, heat the oil in a frying pan. Add the spring onions, almonds, chicken, carrot and mushrooms, and cook over a high heat for about 3–4 minutes, stirring constantly. Reduce the heat and add the cooked noodles and seasoning. Heat through for a further 3–4 minutes. Add the soy sauce and mix well together. Serve at once, garnishing each portion with a spring onion.

Deep-Dish Chicken Pie

Illustrated on the jacket
Serves 6

Metric		Imperial
65 g	**butter or block margarine**	$2\frac{1}{2}$ oz
50 g	**lard**	2 oz
175 g	**plain flour**	6 oz
2.5 ml	**salt**	$\frac{1}{2}$ teaspoon
25 g	***Kellogg's Corn Flakes*, finely crushed**	1 oz
10 ml	**lemon juice**	2 teaspoons
75 ml	**cold water (approximately)**	5 tablespoons
	Filling	
225 g	**carrots, thinly sliced**	8 oz
225 g	**potatoes, thinly sliced**	8 oz
225 g	**button onions, boiled**	8 oz
75 g	**peas**	3 oz
450 g	**cooked chicken, diced**	1 lb
1 (298-g) can	**condensed mushroom soup**	1 ($10\frac{1}{2}$-oz) can
150 ml	**milk**	$\frac{1}{4}$ pint
1.25 ml	**dried thyme**	$\frac{1}{4}$ teaspoon
	salt and pepper	

Put the butter and lard into the freezer or ice compartment of the refrigerator for 30 minutes. In a large bowl, mix together the flour, salt and *Corn Flakes*. Coarsely grate the chilled fats into the flour and mix with a knife until the fat is coated with flour. Add the lemon juice and enough cold water to mix to a soft but not sticky dough. Roll out on a floured surface to a long narrow rectangle 5 mm/$\frac{1}{4}$ inch thick, and mark into three sections with a knife. Fold the top third of the pastry down over the middle third, then fold the bottom third up over this. Quarter turn the pastry, so that the fold is to the left, and roll out again to a rectangle. Repeat this folding and rolling three times, then fold again and place the pastry in a polythene bag. Chill in the refrigerator while preparing the filling.

Put the carrot, potato, onions, peas and chicken into a 2.25-litre/4-pint ovenproof pie dish fitted with a pie funnel. Mix together the soup, milk, thyme and seasoning and pour over the chicken mixture. Roll out the pastry and use to cover the dish, making a small hole in the centre for steam to escape. Flute the edges and decorate the pie with pastry shapes, if liked. Brush with beaten egg and bake at 220°C, 425°F, Gas Mark 7 for 10 minutes, then 160°C, 325°F, Gas Mark 3 for a further 40–50 minutes.

Pineapple Ham Loaf

Illustrated opposite
Serves 6

Metric		Imperial
75 g	***Kellogg's 30% Bran Flakes***	3 oz
150 ml	**milk**	$\frac{1}{4}$ pint
1	**egg, beaten**	1
450 g	**ham, minced**	1 lb
450 g	**freshly minced pork**	1 lb
1	**small onion, finely chopped**	1
$\frac{1}{2}$	**small green pepper, deseeded and finely chopped**	$\frac{1}{2}$
2.5 ml	**salt**	$\frac{1}{2}$ teaspoon
1.25 ml	**pepper**	$\frac{1}{4}$ teaspoon
10 ml	**prepared mustard**	2 teaspoons
50 g	**brown sugar**	2 oz
1 (227-g) can	**pineapple slices, drained (reserve the syrup for the sauce)**	1 (8-oz) can
	Sauce	
	reserved pineapple syrup	
25 ml	**cornflour**	5 teaspoons
50 g	**brown sugar**	2 oz
45 ml	**malt vinegar**	3 tablespoons
5 ml	**prepared mustard**	1 teaspoon

Mix the *30% Bran Flakes* with the milk and leave to stand for 5 minutes. Add the egg, ham, pork, onion, green pepper, seasoning and mustard and mix well together. Press evenly into an ungreased 20-cm/8-inch square baking tin and sprinkle with the sugar. Arrange the pineapple slices on top and bake in a moderate oven (180°C, 350°F, Gas Mark 4) for 1 hour. Serve hot with the sweet and sour sauce or cold.

To make the sauce, add enough water to the pineapple syrup to make up to 300 ml/$\frac{1}{2}$ pint. Mix together the cornflour and brown sugar and gradually add the pineapple juice, stirring continuously. Mix in the vinegar and mustard and transfer to a saucepan. Bring to the boil over a moderate heat, stirring, and simmer gently for 1 minute, until thickened.

Kebabs with tomato rice (see page 52), Pineapple ham loaf (see above).

Kebabs with Tomato Rice

Illustrated on page 51
Serves 4

Metric		Imperial
225 g	**lean lamb, cut from the leg or shoulder**	8 oz
4	**chipolata sausages**	4
8	**button onions**	8
1	**small green pepper**	1
2	**large tomatoes, halved**	2
8	**button mushrooms**	8
	oil	
	Tomato Rice	
225 g (2 bags)	***Kellogg's Boil-in-the-bag Rice***	8 oz (2 bags)
15 g	**butter or margarine**	$\frac{1}{2}$ oz
1	**medium onion, chopped**	1
1 (396-g) can	**peeled tomatoes**	1 (14-oz) can
	salt and pepper	

Cut the lamb into 2.5-cm/1-inch cubes. Carefully twist the sausages in half. Put the peeled onions into a saucepan, cover with water and bring to the boil. Cut the top off the green pepper, discard the seeds and cut into 2.5-cm/1-inch squares. Add to the onions, simmer gently for 5 minutes and then drain.

Thread the lamb, sausages, onions, pepper, tomatoes and mushrooms on to four long kebab skewers, and brush with oil. Place under a preheated grill for about 15 minutes, turning frequently and brushing regularly with oil, until the lamb is cooked.

Meanwhile, cook the rice according to packet instructions. Drain. Melt the butter in a saucepan and fry the onion until tender but not brown. Add the tomatoes and bring to the boil, stirring to break them up. Stir in the cooked rice and mix well. Heat through and season to taste. Turn the tomato rice on to a serving dish and arrange the kebabs on top.

Pork Chops with Tangy Orange Sauce

Serves 4

Metric		Imperial
4	**pork loin chops**	4
1–2	**cloves garlic, crushed**	1–2
	salt and freshly ground black pepper	
	Sauce	
300 ml	***Kellogg's Rise & Shine* Orange (made up)**	$\frac{1}{2}$ pint
1	**onion, finely sliced**	1
	salt and pepper	
15 ml	**cornflour**	1 tablespoon
30 ml	**vinegar**	2 tablespoons
	Garnish	
15 ml	**flaked almonds, toasted**	1 tablespoon
	orange slices	
	sprigs of watercress	

Place the chops in a roasting tin. Sprinkle over the garlic and seasoning and bake in a moderately hot oven (200°C, 400°F, Gas Mark 6) for about 30 minutes.

Pour the *Rise & Shine* into a saucepan. Add the onion and seasoning, bring to the boil then cover and simmer over a low heat for 20 minutes. Blend the cornflour with the vinegar and stir into the pan. Bring back to the boil, stirring, and simmer for a further 5 minutes.

Transfer the chops to a heated serving dish and spoon a little sauce over the top. Sprinkle with the almonds and garnish with orange slices and sprigs of watercress. Serve the remaining sauce separately.

Chilli con Carne

Illustrated opposite
Serves 4–6

Metric		Imperial
450 g	**freshly minced beef**	1 lb
1	**large onion, sliced**	1
1	**small green pepper, deseeded and chopped**	1
50 g	***Kellogg's All-Bran or Bran Buds***	2 oz
1 (432-g) can	**red kidney beans, undrained**	1 (15$\frac{1}{4}$-oz) can
1 (396-g) can	**peeled tomatoes**	1 (14-oz) can
150 ml	**water**	$\frac{1}{4}$ pint
10 ml	**chilli powder**	2 teaspoons
1.25 ml	**garlic powder (optional)**	$\frac{1}{4}$ teaspoon
5 ml	**sugar**	1 teaspoon
1	**bay leaf**	1
30 ml	**tomato purée**	2 tablespoons
	salt	

Put the minced beef into a large saucepan and cook until the meat is browned. Add the onion and green pepper and cook for a few minutes, stirring. Mix in all the remaining ingredients. Cover the pan and cook gently, stirring occasionally, for 1 hour. Remove the bay leaf before serving.

To freeze, cool quickly by standing the pan in a bowl of cold water, then pack into rigid containers. Freeze quickly. To serve, thaw overnight in the refrigerator, then turn into a large saucepan and heat gently, stirring occasionally, for about 20 minutes, or until heated through.

Spicy meatballs (see page 56), Chilli con carne (see above).

Spicy Meatballs

Illustrated on page 55
Serves 4–6

Metric		Imperial
1	**egg**	1
25 g	***Kellogg's Rice Krispies***	1 oz
1	**medium onion, finely chopped**	1
50 g	**dried milk powder**	2 oz
30 ml	**tomato ketchup**	2 tablespoons
5 ml	**salt**	1 teaspoon
	pepper	
450 g	**freshly minced beef**	1 lb
	Sauce	
2 (227-g) cans	**tomato sauce**	2 (8-oz) cans
75 ml	**tomato ketchup**	5 tablespoons
50 g	**brown sugar**	2 oz
1	**medium onion, finely chopped**	1
45 ml	**chutney**	3 tablespoons
30 ml	**Worcestershire sauce**	2 tablespoons
15 ml	**vinegar**	1 tablespoon
1.25 ml	**pepper**	$\frac{1}{4}$ teaspoon

Combine the first eight ingredients in a large bowl and shape into walnut-sized balls. Place in a single layer in a baking tin and cook in a moderately hot oven (200°C, 400°F, Gas Mark 6) for 10–12 minutes, until well browned. Meanwhile, put the ingredients for the sauce into a large pan. Cover and cook over a low heat for 15 minutes, then add the meatballs and cook for a further 10 minutes. Serve with *Kellogg's Boil-in-the-bag Rice*.

Crunchy Shepherd's Squares

Serves 6

Metric		Imperial
50 g	**Kellogg's Corn Flakes, crushed**	2 oz
5 ml	salt	1 teaspoon
1.25 ml	pepper	$\frac{1}{4}$ teaspoon
15 ml	prepared mustard	1 tablespoon
75 ml	milk	5 tablespoons
450 g	freshly minced beef	1 lb
2 (64-g) packets	instant mashed potato	2 (2.26-oz) packets
2	eggs, beaten	2
$\frac{1}{2}$	small onion, finely chopped	$\frac{1}{2}$
10 ml	dried parsley flakes	2 teaspoons
25 g	butter	1 oz
50 g	Cheddar cheese, grated	2 oz

Measure half the *Corn Flakes* with the salt, pepper, mustard and milk into a bowl. Add the mince and mix well. Spread evenly into a Swiss roll tin. Make up the instant potato. Add the eggs, onion and parsley and mix well. Spread over the meat and cook at 180°C, 350°F, Gas Mark 4 for 35 minutes. Meanwhile melt the butter and stir into the remaining *Corn Flakes*. Sprinkle the cheese evenly over the potato and top with the *Corn Flakes*. Return to the oven and cook for a further 10 minutes.

Curried Pilaf

Illustrated on page 59
Serves 4

Metric		Imperial
100 g (1 bag)	**Kellogg's Boil-in-the-bag Rice**	4 oz (1 bag)
225 g	onions, chopped	8 oz
50 g	butter	2 oz
225 g	cooked chicken, diced	8 oz
225 g	luncheon meat, diced	8 oz
5 ml	curry powder	1 teaspoon
30 ml	sweet pickle	2 tablespoons

Cook the rice. Fry the onions in the butter until tender, then stir in the rice and remaining ingredients. Heat through for 10 minutes.

Savoury Tongue Rolls

Illustrated opposite
Serves 6

Metric		Imperial
100 g (1 bag)	***Kellogg's Boil-in-the-bag Rice***	4 oz (1 bag)
1 (213-g) can	**peach slices, drained**	1 (7½-oz) can
2	**sticks celery, chopped**	2
75 g	**nuts or sultanas**	3 oz
45 ml	**mayonnaise**	3 tablespoons
10 ml	**Worcestershire sauce**	2 teaspoons
	juice of ½ lemon	
	salt and pepper	
7.5 ml	**prepared English mustard**	1½ teaspoons
6	**slices tongue**	6

Cook the rice, drain and cool. Chop the peaches (reserving six slices) and mix with the rice, celery, nuts, mayonnaise, Worcestershire sauce, lemon juice and seasoning. Spread mustard thinly on each tongue slice and divide the rice mixture between them. Roll up and decorate with the reserved peach slices.

Savoury Rice

Illustrated opposite
Serves 2–3

Metric		Imperial
100 g (1 bag)	***Kellogg's Boil-in-the-bag Rice***	4 oz (1 bag)
25 g	**butter**	1 oz
1	**onion, chopped**	1
1	**green pepper, chopped**	1
2	**sticks celery, chopped**	2
4	**rashers streaky bacon, chopped**	4

Cook the rice and drain. Melt the butter and sauté the onion, pepper, celery and bacon for 5 minutes. Add the rice for a further 5 minutes.

Savoury tongue rolls (see above), Curried pilaf (see page 57), Stuffed onions (see page 60), Savoury rice (see above).

Stuffed Onions

Illustrated on page 59
Serves 4

Metric		Imperial
100 g (1 bag)	***Kellogg's Boil-in-the-bag Rice***	4 oz (1 bag)
4	**large onions, peeled**	4
1	**medium onion, chopped**	1
15 g	**lard**	$\frac{1}{2}$ oz
450 g	**freshly minced beef**	1 lb
1	**beef stock cube, crumbled**	1
30 ml	**boiling water**	2 tablespoons
30 ml	**tomato purée**	2 tablespoons
5 ml	**prepared mustard**	1 teaspoon
2.5 ml	**dried mixed herbs**	$\frac{1}{2}$ teaspoon

Cook the rice and drain. Simmer the whole onions in boiling water for 5 minutes. Drain. Scoop out the centre of each onion. Fry the chopped onion in the lard until tender. Add the beef and brown quickly. Stir in the remaining ingredients and season to taste. Sprinkle the inside of each onion with salt, then stuff with the mince mixture. Stand in an ovenproof dish, cover with foil and bake at 180°C, 350°F, Gas Mark 4 for 1 hour. Accompany with sweetcorn.

Indian Noodles

Serves 2

Metric		Imperial
1 (100-g) packet	***Kellogg's Super Noodles* Mild Curry Flavour**	1 ($3\frac{1}{2}$-oz) packet
2	**sticks celery, chopped**	2
25 g	**sultanas**	1 oz
3	**eggs, hard-boiled and quartered**	3
30 ml	**yogurt**	2 tablespoons
	salt and pepper	

Cook the noodles, adding the celery and sultanas. Gently stir in the eggs, yogurt and seasoning and heat through.

Noodles Romanoff

Serves 2

Metric		Imperial
1 (100-g) packet	***Kellogg's Super Noodles* Barbecue Flavour**	1 (3½-oz) packet
1	**large clove garlic, crushed**	1
1 (142-ml) carton	**soured cream**	1 (5-fl oz) carton
30 ml	**grated Parmesan cheese**	2 tablespoons
10 ml	**chopped chives**	2 teaspoons
¼	**green pepper, finely chopped**	¼
	salt and pepper	

Make up the noodles according to packet instructions. Stir in the garlic, soured cream, Parmesan, chives, green pepper and seasoning. Cook over a gentle heat for 1 minute and serve sprinkled with extra Parmesan.

Crunchy Topping

Makes 25 g/1 oz topping

Metric		Imperial
15 g	**butter or margarine**	½ oz
25 g	***Kellogg's Rice Krispies***	1 oz

Melt the butter in a small frying pan over a low heat. Remove from the heat, add the *Rice Krispies* and stir until well coated. Spoon over the top of a vegetable or main dish casserole before baking.

Or cook the *Rice Krispies* in the butter until crisp and lightly browned. Remove from the heat and sprinkle over soups or salads.

Variations

Stir any of the following into the melted butter before adding the cereal.

generous pinch	**garlic or onion salt**	generous pinch
1.25 ml	**chilli or curry powder**	¼ teaspoon
5 ml	**Worcestershire sauce**	1 teaspoon

Either of the following may be tossed into the crisped cereal.

15 ml	**dried parsley flakes**	1 tablespoon
15 ml	**grated Parmesan cheese**	1 tablespoon

Vegetables and Salads

You don't have to be vegetarian to enjoy the vegetable and salad recipes in this section. Fresh vegetables, root, green or salad, should form an important part of your daily diet, and recipes incorporating cereals make delicious dishes high in natural fibre and vitamins.
The salad recipes here show how easy it is to make quick, economical and imaginative salads to delight both family and guests, simply by using interesting combinations of ingredients and careful seasoning.

Carrots au Gratin

Illustrated opposite
Serves 6

Metric		Imperial
65 g	**butter or margarine**	$2\frac{1}{2}$ oz
25 g	***Kellogg's Corn Flakes*, crushed**	1 oz
1	**small onion, chopped**	1
45 ml	**plain flour**	3 tablespoons
5 ml	**salt**	1 teaspoon
	pepper	
450 ml	**milk**	$\frac{3}{4}$ pint
100 g	**Cheddar cheese, grated**	4 oz
675 g	**carrots, sliced and cooked**	$1\frac{1}{2}$ lb
15 ml	**dried parsley flakes**	1 tablespoon

Melt 25 g/1 oz butter. Add to the *Corn Flakes* and mix well. Set aside for the topping. Melt the remaining butter in a saucepan, add the onion and cook gently until soft but not browned. Stir in the flour, salt and pepper. Remove from the heat and gradually stir in the milk. Return to the heat and bring to the boil, stirring. Add the cheese and, when melted, remove from the heat. Stir in the carrots and parsley flakes. Spread the mixture into a large gratin dish and sprinkle the *Corn Flakes* over the top. Bake in a moderate oven (180°C, 350°F, Gas Mark 4) for 20 minutes.

Crispy potato croquettes (see page 64), Carrots au gratin (see above), Cauliflower bake with bran topping (see page 65).

Crispy Potato Croquettes

Illustrated on page 63
Serves 4–6

Metric		Imperial
1	**egg, separated**	1
5 ml	**chopped parsley**	1 teaspoon
450 g	**very stiff mashed potato**	1 lb
50 g	***Kellogg's Corn Flakes*, finely crushed**	2 oz
25 g	**butter or margarine, melted**	1 oz

Mix the egg yolk and parsley together. Add the potato and mix until well blended. In a small shallow dish, beat the egg white with a fork until foamy. Shape the potato mixture into 20–24 balls, each about 2.5 cm/1 inch in diameter. Dip the balls in the egg white then coat with crushed *Corn Flakes*. Place on a well greased baking tray and spoon a little melted butter over each ball. Bake in a hot oven (230°C, 450°F, Gas Mark 8) for about 10 minutes, until lightly browned and crisp.

To freeze, cool quickly and open freeze. When frozen, pack in polythene bags or rigid containers. To serve, place the frozen potato balls on a baking tray and heat in a moderately hot oven (190°C, 375°F, Gas Mark 5) for 15–20 minutes, until warmed through.

Cheese and Vegetable Medley

Serves 4

Metric		Imperial
100 g (1 bag)	***Kellogg's Boil-in-the-bag Rice***	4 oz (1 bag)
1 (227-g) packet	**frozen mixed vegetables**	1 (8-oz) packet
3	**eggs, hard-boiled**	3
100 g	**Cheddar cheese, grated**	4 oz
2	**tomatoes, sliced**	2

Cook the rice according to packet instructions. Drain well. Cook the vegetables according to packet instructions then drain and mix with the rice. Turn half the rice mixture into a well buttered 1.25-litre/2-pint flameproof dish. Slice the eggs and arrange over the rice, then cover with the remaining rice. Sprinkle over the cheese and top with the sliced tomatoes. Place under a preheated grill until the cheese has melted and the tomatoes are cooked.

Cauliflower Bake with Bran Topping

Illustrated on page 63
Serves 4–6

Metric		Imperial
1	**medium cauliflower**	1
25 g	**butter or margarine**	1 oz
1	**large onion, sliced**	1
1	**small red pepper, deseeded and chopped**	1
25 g	**plain flour**	1 oz
150 ml	**chicken stock, made from a cube**	$\frac{1}{4}$ pint
300 ml	**milk**	$\frac{1}{2}$ pint
	salt and pepper	
	Topping	
25 g	**butter or margarine, melted**	1 oz
25 g	***Kellogg's All-Bran* or *Bran Buds***	1 oz
1.25 ml	**garlic salt**	$\frac{1}{4}$ teaspoon

Break the cauliflower into florets and cook in boiling salted water for about 10 minutes, until almost tender. Drain well.

Melt the butter in a large saucepan, add the onion and cook until soft but not browned. Stir in the red pepper and the flour and cook for a minute. Remove from the heat and gradually stir in the stock and milk. Return to the heat, bring to the boil, stirring constantly, and cook for a minute. Add the cauliflower and season to taste. Turn into a 1.75-litre/3-pint ovenproof dish.

Mix together the ingredients for the topping and sprinkle over the cauliflower. Bake in a moderate oven (180°C, 350°F, Gas Mark 4) for about 20 minutes, until heated through.

Vegetable Bran Bread

Illustrated opposite
Makes 1 loaf

Metric		Imperial
25 g	**butter or margarine**	1 oz
100 g	**onions, finely chopped**	4 oz
100 g	**carrots, grated**	4 oz
100 g	***Kellogg's All-Bran* or *Bran Buds***	4 oz
150 ml	**milk**	$\frac{1}{4}$ pint
5 ml	**sugar**	1 teaspoon
150 ml	**warm water (37°C/100°F)**	$\frac{1}{4}$ pint
15 g	**dried yeast**	$\frac{1}{2}$ oz
350 g	**plain flour**	12 oz
10 ml	**salt**	2 teaspoons

Melt the butter in a small saucepan. Add the onion and carrot and cook gently, covered, until tender but not brown. Allow to cool. Put the *All-Bran* and milk into a mixing bowl and leave until softened. Dissolve the sugar in the water, stir in the yeast and allow to stand until the yeast is frothy. Stir into the *All-Bran* mixture. Sift the flour and salt together and add to the *All-Bran* mixture with the cooled carrot and onion. Mix to a firm dough then knead for about 5 minutes, until the dough is elastic. Place in a greased 1-kg/2-lb loaf tin and cover with greased polythene. Leave in a warm place until the dough has risen to the top of the tin, about 40 minutes.

Bake the loaf in a hot oven (220°C, 425°F, Gas Mark 7) for 10 minutes, then reduce to moderately hot (200°C, 400°F, Gas Mark 6) for a further 30–40 minutes. Cover lightly with foil during the last 10 minutes cooking if the loaf is browning too much on top. Turn out and cool on a wire rack. Use to make open sandwiches.

Vegetable bran bread (see above), Sardine and egg open sandwiches, Garlic sausage and cottage cheese open sandwiches (see page 68).

Sardine and Egg Open Sandwiches

Illustrated on page 67
Serves 2

Metric		Imperial
2 slices	**Vegetable Bran Bread (see page 66)**	2 slices
	softened butter to spread	
	crisp lettuce leaves	
1 (120-g) can	**sardines in oil, drained**	1 ($4\frac{1}{4}$-oz) can
2	**hard-boiled egg slices**	2
2	**tomato slices**	2
	mayonnaise or salad cream	
	chopped parsley to garnish	

Spread the bread with butter and cover with lettuce leaves. Place the sardines on the lettuce then arrange slices of egg and tomato in the centre. Spoon mayonnaise over the top and sprinkle with chopped parsley.

Garlic Sausage and Cottage Cheese Open Sandwiches

Illustrated on page 67
Serves 2

Metric		Imperial
2 slices	**Vegetable Bran Bread (see page 66)**	2 slices
	softened butter to spread	
50 g	**garlic sausage, thinly sliced**	2 oz
	cucumber slices	
50 g	**cottage cheese**	2 oz
2	**radishes**	2
	chopped chives to garnish	

Spread the bread with butter and place the sliced garlic sausage on top. Arrange the cucumber slices in a ring and pile cottage cheese in the centre. Cut the radishes into water lilies or slices and place on top of the cottage cheese. Sprinkle with chopped chives to serve.

Lentil Rissoles with Tomato Sauce

Illustrated on page 71
Serves 4

Metric		Imperial
100 g	**lentils, soaked overnight**	4 oz
1	**onion, finely chopped**	1
25 g	***Kellogg's All-Bran* or *Bran Buds***	1 oz
50 g	**fresh white breadcrumbs**	2 oz
15 ml	**tomato purée**	1 tablespoon
	salt and pepper	
5 ml	**dried sage**	1 teaspoon
1	**egg, beaten**	1
	beaten egg to coat	
	dried breadcrumbs to coat	
	oil to deep fry	
	Sauce	
1	**onion, finely chopped**	1
30 ml	**oil**	2 tablespoons
15 g	**plain flour**	$\frac{1}{2}$ oz
300 ml	**stock**	$\frac{1}{2}$ pint
1 (227-g) can	**peeled tomatoes**	1 (8-oz) can
15 ml	**tomato ketchup**	1 tablespoon
	salt and pepper	

Cook the lentils in water to cover for about 30–40 minutes, or until tender. Drain. Mix the lentils, onion, *All-Bran*, breadcrumbs, tomato purée, seasoning, sage and egg together. Leave to stand for 30 minutes. Shape the mixture into eight balls, dip each in beaten egg and coat in breadcrumbs.

To make the sauce, lightly fry the onion in the oil until tender. Stir in the flour and cook for a minute. Remove from the heat and blend in the stock and tomatoes. Return to the heat and bring to the boil, stirring. Add the tomato ketchup and seasoning to taste. Place the sauce in a blender and liquidise until smooth. Return to the pan and heat through.

Fry the rissoles in deep hot oil for 5 minutes. Drain on kitchen paper and serve with the tomato sauce.

Note This recipe is suitable for vegetarians.

Baked Onion Parcels

Illustrated opposite
Serves 4

Metric		Imperial
4	**large onions**	4
1 (227-g) packet	**frozen chopped spinach, thawed**	1 (8-oz) packet
25 g	***Kellogg's All-Bran* or *Bran Buds***	1 oz
2	**eggs, hard-boiled and chopped**	2
	salt	
1 (227-g) packet	**shortcrust pastry mix**	1 (8-oz) packet
	milk to glaze	

Cook the peeled onions in boiling water for 10 minutes. Drain and cool. Scoop out the centres with a small spoon and save for another recipe. To make the stuffing, mix the spinach, *All-Bran*, egg and salt together. Use to fill the onions.

Make up the pastry mix according to packet instructions and roll out into four 15-cm/6-inch squares. Place an onion in the centre of each pastry square, moisten the edges and bring the four corners to the top of the onion, sealing all edges well. Place on a baking tray. Brush the onion parcels with a little milk and bake in a moderate oven (180°C, 350°F, Gas Mark 4) for 45 minutes. Serve hot.

Note This recipe is suitable for vegetarians.

Grapefruit cheesecake (see page 77), Baked onion parcels (see above), Cheese and onion loaf (see page 72), Lentil rissoles with tomato sauce (see page 69).

Cheese and Onion Loaf

Illustrated on page 71
Serves 6

Metric		Imperial
50 g	***Kellogg's All-Bran* or *Bran Buds***	2 oz
150 ml	**milk**	$\frac{1}{4}$ pint
225 g	**self-raising flour**	8 oz
pinch	**salt**	pinch
pinch	**cayenne pepper**	pinch
50 g	**margarine**	2 oz
100 g	**cheese, grated**	4 oz
1	**onion, chopped and lightly fried**	1
	tomato slices to garnish	

Soak the *All-Bran* in the milk until the milk is absorbed. Sift the flour, salt and cayenne into a mixing bowl. Rub in the margarine then stir in the cheese and onion. Add the *All-Bran* and mix thoroughly. Turn out and knead on a lightly floured board. Press the mixture into a greased 0.5-kg/1-lb loaf tin and bake in a moderately hot oven (190°C, 375°F, Gas Mark 5) for about 50 minutes.

Turn out and eat warm or cold, garnished with tomato slices.

Note This recipe is suitable for vegetarians.

Tuna and Prawn Salad

Illustrated on the jacket
Serves 4

Metric		Imperial
100 g (1 bag)	**Kellogg's Boil-in-the-bag Rice**	4 oz (1 bag)
1 (198-g) can	**tuna, drained**	1 (7-oz) can
100 g	**peeled prawns**	4 oz
$\frac{1}{2}$	**small cucumber**	$\frac{1}{2}$
60 ml	**mayonnaise**	4 tablespoons
1.25 ml	**Tabasco sauce**	$\frac{1}{4}$ teaspoon
	juice of $\frac{1}{2}$ lemon	
50 g	**seedless raisins**	2 oz
50 g	**shelled walnuts, chopped**	2 oz
1	**red pepper, deseeded and chopped**	1
	salt and pepper	
2	**tomatoes, cut into wedges**	2

Cook the rice according to packet instructions. Drain and rinse in cold water, then allow to drain thoroughly. Leave until cold. Flake the tuna roughly with a fork and mix in half the prawns. Cut eight thin slices of cucumber and reserve for garnish. Dice the remaining cucumber and add to the fish with the rice, mayonnaise, Tabasco, lemon juice, raisins, walnuts and red pepper. Mix well and season to taste. Turn into a salad bowl or serving dish and garnish with the remaining prawns, sliced cucumber and tomato wedges. Chill before serving.

Green Bean and Onion Salad

Illustrated opposite
Serves 6–8

Metric		Imperial
50 g	**butter or margarine**	2 oz
2.5 ml	**garlic salt**	$\frac{1}{2}$ teaspoon
50 g	***Kellogg's All-Bran* or *Bran Buds***	2 oz
450 g	**fresh or frozen green beans, cooked**	1 lb
100 g	**Swiss cheese, cut into strips**	4 oz
	Dressing	
2.5 ml	**salt**	$\frac{1}{2}$ teaspoon
generous pinch	**pepper**	generous pinch
2.5 ml	**dried basil**	$\frac{1}{2}$ teaspoon
2.5 ml	**dry mustard**	$\frac{1}{2}$ teaspoon
45 ml	**vinegar**	3 tablespoons
15 ml	**clear honey**	1 tablespoon
75 ml	**vegetable oil**	5 tablespoons
1	**onion to garnish**	1

Melt the butter in a frying pan. Stir in the garlic salt and *All-Bran*. Cook for 1–2 minutes then set aside. Combine the beans and cheese in a mixing bowl and chill.

Meanwhile mix the salt, pepper, basil, mustard, vinegar and honey in a small bowl, and slowly beat in the oil. Chill.

Slice the onion finely. Just before serving, toss the bean mixture with the *All-Bran* and dressing and garnish with onion slices.

Green bean and onion salad (see above), Lettuce and bacon salad (see page 76).

Lettuce and Bacon Salad

Illustrated on page 75
Serves 6–8

Metric		Imperial
25 g	**butter or margarine**	1 oz
3.75 ml	**paprika pepper**	$\frac{3}{4}$ teaspoon
1.25 ml	**garlic salt**	$\frac{1}{4}$ teaspoon
15 ml	**sesame seeds**	1 tablespoon
50 g	***Kellogg's All-Bran* or *Bran Buds***	2 oz
15 ml	**grated Parmesan cheese**	1 tablespoon
6	**rashers streaky bacon**	6
2	**medium Iceberg or Webbs lettuces**	2
2	**tomatoes, chopped**	2
1	**bunch spring onions, chopped**	1
2.5 ml	**dried oregano**	$\frac{1}{2}$ teaspoon
2.5 ml	**pepper**	$\frac{1}{2}$ teaspoon
45 ml	**vinegar**	3 tablespoons
10 ml	**sugar**	2 teaspoons

Melt the butter or margarine in a frying pan. Stir in the paprika, garlic salt and sesame seeds. Add the *All-Bran* and stir until the butter is absorbed. Remove from the heat and stir in the cheese. Fry the bacon until crisp, drain and reserve the drippings. Crumble the bacon.

Tear the lettuces into bite-sized pieces and toss with the tomatoes, onions, oregano and pepper in a large salad bowl. Combine the bacon drippings, vinegar and sugar in a small pan and bring to the boil. Pour over the lettuce and leave for 1 minute. Sprinkle with the cereal and bacon and serve at once.

Desserts

Hot or cold, a dessert should ideally complement the previous courses to make up part of a well-balanced menu. Light desserts are refreshing after a rich main course, while more filling puddings are ideal to follow a less substantial main meal. In this section are both quick and simple puddings for the family while for the adventurous cook there are desserts of a more exotic nature.
Desserts are popular and need not necessarily be fattening. Fruit desserts are full of vitamins and not too high in calories.

Grapefruit Cheesecake

Illustrated on page 71
Serves 6

Metric		Imperial
75 g	**butter**	3 oz
45 ml	**golden syrup**	3 tablespoons
175 g	***Kellogg's 30% Bran Flakes***	6 oz
	Filling	
15 g	**powdered gelatine**	$\frac{1}{2}$ oz
30 ml	**water**	2 tablespoons
225 g	**cottage cheese, sieved**	8 oz
150 ml	**double cream**	$\frac{1}{4}$ pint
	juice of 1 grapefruit	
25 g	**castor sugar**	1 oz
	grapefruit segments to decorate	

Melt the butter and golden syrup together. Stir in the *30% Bran Flakes* and press over the base and sides of an 18-cm/7-inch flan dish, reserving a little for decoration. Bake at 180°C, 350°F, Gas Mark 4 for 10 minutes. Cool.

Dissolve the gelatine in the water over a pan of hot water and cool slightly. Mix together the cottage cheese, cream, grapefruit juice and sugar. Whisk in the cooled gelatine. When quite thick, turn into the flan dish and spread level. Place in the refrigerator to set. Just before serving, decorate with grapefruit segments and the remaining *30% Bran Flakes* mixture.

Coffee Banana Swirl

Illustrated opposite
Serves 6–8

Metric		Imperial
450 ml	**milk**	$\frac{3}{4}$ pint
2	**eggs, separated**	2
30 ml	**coffee essence**	2 tablespoons
$\frac{1}{2}$ (40-g) packet	***Kellogg's Two Shakes* Banana Flavour**	$\frac{1}{2}$ (1.4-oz) packet
15 ml	**powdered gelatine**	1 tablespoon
45 ml	**cold water**	3 tablespoons
150 ml	**double cream, lightly whipped**	$\frac{1}{4}$ pint
	Decoration	
	whipped cream	
	angelica	

Whisk 150 ml/$\frac{1}{4}$ pint milk, the egg yolks and coffee essence together in a saucepan. Cook over a low heat, stirring, until just beginning to thicken. Strain and leave until cold. Whisk the remaining milk with the Banana *Two Shakes*.

Put half the gelatine with half the water into one bowl and the remaining gelatine and water into a second bowl. Dissolve the gelatine over a pan of hot water, then stir the cold coffee mixture into one bowl and the banana mixture into the other. Leave until the mixtures begin to thicken then fold half the cream into each. Whisk the egg whites until stiff and fold half into each mixture. Spoon alternately into a 1-litre/$1\frac{1}{2}$-pint jelly mould and chill until set. Unmould and decorate with piped whipped cream and angelica.

Coffee banana swirl (see above), Rhubarb russe (see page 80).

Rhubarb Russe

Illustrated on page 79
Serves 6

Metric		Imperial
450 g	**rhubarb**	1 lb
30 ml	**redcurrant jelly**	2 tablespoons
60 ml	**water**	4 tablespoons
15 g	**powdered gelatine**	$\frac{1}{2}$ oz
2	**egg whites**	2
100 g	**castor sugar**	4 oz
300 ml	**double cream**	$\frac{1}{2}$ pint
40 g	***Kellogg's Frosties***	$1\frac{1}{2}$ oz

Wash the rhubarb and cut into 2.5-cm/1-inch lengths. Put the rhubarb, redcurrant jelly and 30 ml/2 tablespoons of the water into a saucepan, cover and cook gently until the rhubarb is tender. Sieve or liquidise the rhubarb and allow to cool. Put the gelatine and remaining water into a bowl over a pan of hot water and stir until the gelatine has dissolved. Stir the rhubarb purée into the gelatine and leave in a cool place until beginning to set.

Whisk the egg whites until stiff, then gradually whisk in the sugar until smooth and glossy peaks form. Whip the cream until soft peaks form, fold into the egg whites, then fold this cream mixture into the rhubarb. Turn into a 15–18-cm/6–7-inch cake tin or charlotte russe mould and refrigerate until set.

Just before serving, dip the mould into warm water and invert on to a flat plate. Press the *Frosties* on to the top and sides of the russe.

To freeze, do not unmould the russe and ensure that the container used is freezer proof. Cover with freezer film and freeze quickly. To serve, unwrap, remove from the mould while still frozen and allow to thaw at room temperature for about 4 hours. Decorate with *Frosties* as above.

American Country Cheesecake

Serves 6–8

Metric		Imperial
40 g	**butter or margarine**	$1\frac{1}{2}$ oz
15 ml	**golden syrup**	1 tablespoon
100 g	***Kellogg's Country Store***	4 oz
	Filling	
175 g	**cream cheese**	6 oz
300 ml	**double cream**	$\frac{1}{2}$ pint
1 packet	***Kellogg's Rise & Shine* Orange**	1 packet
300 ml	**water**	$\frac{1}{2}$ pint
15 g	**powdered gelatine**	$\frac{1}{2}$ oz
1	**large orange**	1
	Decoration	
1	**large orange**	1
	angelica leaves	

Put the butter and golden syrup into a saucepan and heat gently until the butter has melted. Remove from the heat and stir in the *Country Store*, mixing well. Press into the base of a lightly oiled 20-cm/8-inch loose-based cake tin. Leave in a cool place while preparing the filling.

Beat the cream cheese until soft. Gradually stir in the cream and beat or whisk until the mixture thickens. Make up the *Rise & Shine* with the 300 ml/$\frac{1}{2}$ pint water. Place 60 ml/4 tablespoons of the prepared drink in a small bowl and sprinkle over the gelatine. Stand the bowl in a pan of hot water and stir until the gelatine has dissolved. Stir the remaining orange drink into the dissolved gelatine, then gradually stir this into the cream cheese mixture. Cut the peel and pith from the orange and divide into segments. Chop and add to the cream cheese mixture. Leave until beginning to set then pour into the tin. Leave in a cool place until set.

Carefully remove the cheesecake from the tin and slide gently on to a serving plate. Decorate with fresh orange segments and angelica leaves.

To freeze, do not decorate. Slide the cheesecake on to a baking tray covered with a piece of freezer film. Freeze quickly, then wrap completely in film and overwrap with foil. When required, unwrap and place on a serving plate. Cover loosely with a polythene bag and thaw at room temperature for 6–8 hours. Decorate as above.

Country Trifles

Illustrated opposite
Serves 4

Metric		Imperial
$\frac{1}{2}$	**strawberry or raspberry jelly**	$\frac{1}{2}$
1 (213-g) can	**fruit cocktail**	1 ($7\frac{1}{2}$-oz) can
75 g	***Kellogg's Country Store***	3 oz
30 ml	**custard powder**	2 tablespoons
30 ml	**sugar**	2 tablespoons
568 ml	**milk**	1 pint
	Topping	
150 ml	**double cream**	$\frac{1}{4}$ pint
25 g	***Kellogg's Country Store***	1 oz
2	**glacé cherries, halved**	2

Dissolve the jelly in 150 ml/$\frac{1}{4}$ pint boiling water, then add the syrup from the can of fruit cocktail and enough water to make up to 300 ml/$\frac{1}{2}$ pint. Divide the fruit cocktail and *Country Store* between four individual sundae glasses. Pour over the jelly and leave in a cool place until set.

Mix the custard powder and sugar with a little of the milk, and heat the remaining milk until almost boiling. Stir into the custard mixture, then return to the heat and bring to the boil, stirring constantly. Cook for a minute, until smooth and thickened, then cover with a piece of wet greaseproof paper and leave to cool. When the custard is almost cold, pour it over the set jelly and spread level. Chill until firm.

Whip the cream until stiff and pipe or spoon around the edge of each glass, on top of the custard. Pile *Country Store* in the centre and top each trifle with a halved cherry.

Country trifles (see above), Cream and pineapple squares (see page 84).

Cream and Pineapple Squares

Illustrated on page 83
Makes 9

Metric		Imperial
1 packet	**Kellogg's Rise & Shine Pineapple**	1 packet
300 ml	**water**	$\frac{1}{2}$ pint
15 g	**powdered gelatine**	$\frac{1}{2}$ oz
350 g	**cream cheese**	12 oz
3	**eggs, separated**	3
150 ml	**double cream, lightly whipped**	$\frac{1}{4}$ pint
	Decoration	
	whipped cream	
9	**macaroons, halved**	9
	melted chocolate	

Make up the *Rise & Shine* using the 300 ml/$\frac{1}{2}$ pint water. Put the gelatine and 45 ml/3 tablespoons of the pineapple drink into a small bowl. Place over a pan of boiling water and stir until the gelatine has dissolved. Pour the dissolved gelatine into the remaining pineapple drink and leave to set until slightly thickened.

Whisk the cream cheese and egg yolks together, then whisk in the setting jelly. Fold in the lightly whipped cream. Whisk the egg whites until stiff and fold into the jelly. Turn the mixture into a lightly wetted deep 18-cm/7-inch square tin and allow to set in the refrigerator.

Turn out on to a serving plate, dipping the tin into warm water if necessary. Cut the square into nine small squares and pipe a blob of whipped cream on top of each. Arrange two macaroon halves on each like a butterfly and finally trickle over a little cooled melted chocolate.

Lemon and Grapefruit Snow

Illustrated on the jacket
Serves 4–5

Metric		Imperial
300 ml	***Kellogg's Rise & Shine* Grapefruit** (made up)	$\frac{1}{2}$ pint
1	**lemon jelly**	1
2	**egg whites**	2

Heat the *Rise & Shine*, add the lemon jelly and stir until the jelly has dissolved. Cool. When the jelly is nearly set, whisk until double in volume. Whisk the egg whites until stiff and fold into the whisked jelly. Pour into individual serving glasses and chill for about 15 minutes. Decorate, if liked, with whipped cream and angelica.

Pear and Lemon Jelly

Serves 6

Metric		Imperial
450 g	**pears**	1 lb
150 ml	**water**	$\frac{1}{4}$ pint
1 packet	***Kellogg's Rise & Shine* Lemon**	1 packet
25 g	**powdered gelatine**	1 oz

Quarter, peel and core the pears. Put the pear quarters and water into a small frying pan. Cover tightly and simmer gently for 10–15 minutes, until the pears are tender. Remove the pears with a draining spoon and pour the cooking liquor into a measuring jug. Liquidise or sieve the pears. Make the reserved cooking liquor up to 600 ml/1 pint with cold water and use to make up the *Rise & Shine* as directed on the packet.

Put the gelatine into a small bowl with 30 ml/2 tablespoons cold water and stir over a pan of hot water until dissolved. Remove from the heat, add the pear purée then stir in the *Rise & Shine*. Mix well. Pour into a wetted 1–1.25-litre/1$\frac{1}{2}$–2-pint jelly mould, or six individual jelly moulds and leave in the refrigerator until set. To unmould, dip the mould into hot water and turn out on to a serving plate.

Festive Pie

Illustrated opposite and on the jacket
Serves 6–8

Metric		Imperial
50 g	**butter or margarine**	2 oz
45 ml	**golden syrup**	3 tablespoons
100 g	**plain chocolate**	4 oz
50 g	***Kellogg's Rice Krispies***	2 oz
	Filling	
350 g	**cream cheese**	12 oz
50 g	**castor sugar**	2 oz
30 ml	**brandy (optional)**	2 tablespoons
100 g	**maraschino cherries, quartered**	4 oz
100 g	**blanched almonds, chopped**	4 oz
150 ml	**double cream, lightly whipped**	$\frac{1}{4}$ pint

toasted slivered almonds to decorate

Melt the butter, golden syrup and chocolate together in a pan. Remove from the heat and stir in the *Rice Krispies*, coating them thoroughly. Use to line the base and sides of a 23-cm/9-inch flan dish and chill.

In a large bowl beat the cream cheese until smooth, stir in the remaining ingredients and pile into the flan dish. Either leave the surface rough or smooth over. Freeze for at least 4 hours and decorate with toasted slivered almonds just before serving, if liked.

Orange Dessert

Serves 2

Metric		Imperial
75 g	***Kellogg's Country Store***	3 oz
1 (150-g) carton	**orange yogurt**	1 (5.3-oz) carton
60 ml	**milk**	4 tablespoons
1	**orange, segmented**	1

Mix together the *Country Store*, yogurt and milk, turn into serving dishes and decorate with the orange segments.

Lime delight (see page 88), Festive pie (see above).

Lime Delight

Illustrated on page 87
Serves 6–8

Metric		Imperial
150 g	**plain flour**	5 oz
2.5 ml	**salt**	$\frac{1}{2}$ teaspoon
15 ml	**castor sugar**	1 tablespoon
50 g	***Kellogg's Corn Flakes*, finely crushed**	2 oz
60 ml	**vegetable oil**	4 tablespoons
30 ml	**cold water**	2 tablespoons
	Filling	
300 ml	**double cream**	$\frac{1}{2}$ pint
1 (397-g) can	**sweetened condensed milk**	1 (14-oz) can
90 ml	**fresh lime juice**	6 tablespoons
few drops	**green food colouring (optional)**	few drops
3.75 ml	**finely grated lime rind (optional)**	$\frac{3}{4}$ teaspoon
	lime slices to decorate	

Put the flour, salt, sugar and crushed *Corn Flakes* into a mixing bowl. Add the oil and water, stirring with a fork until well mixed. Turn into a deep 20–23-cm/8–9-inch pie plate and, using the back of a spoon, press evenly and firmly over the base and sides. Prick all over with a fork. Bake in a hot oven (230°C, 450°F, Gas Mark 8) for 10 minutes, or until lightly browned. Cool completely.

Whip the cream until it stands in stiff peaks. Put the sweetened condensed milk into a mixing bowl and gradually add the lime juice, stirring constantly. Stir in the food colouring and lime rind, then fold in three-quarters of the whipped cream. Turn into the prepared case, swirl the surface, and chill for about 2 hours, until firm. Decorate with the remaining whipped cream and lime slices.

French Cherry Dessert

Serves 6–9

Metric		Imperial
125 g	**butter or margarine**	4 oz
45 ml	**icing sugar, sifted**	3 tablespoons
75 g	**self-raising flour**	3 oz
40 g	***Kellogg's Corn Flakes*, crushed**	$1\frac{1}{2}$ oz
	Topping	
25 g	**self-raising flour**	1 oz
2.5 ml	**baking powder**	$\frac{1}{2}$ teaspoon
1.25 ml	**salt**	$\frac{1}{4}$ teaspoon
2	**eggs**	2
225 g	**granulated sugar**	8 oz
5 ml	**vanilla essence**	1 teaspoon
75 g	**shelled walnuts, chopped**	3 oz
50 g	**desiccated coconut**	2 oz
1 (226-g) jar	**maraschino cherries, drained and chopped**	1 (8-oz) jar

Put the margarine and icing sugar into a bowl and beat until smooth. Stir in the flour and crushed *Corn Flakes*. Spread this mixture over the base of a 20-cm/8-inch square cake tin and bake in a moderate oven (160°C, 325°F, Gas Mark 3) for 20 minutes. Remove from the oven.

Mix together the flour, baking powder and salt. Beat the eggs and stir in the sugar and vanilla essence. Add the flour and mix well then stir in the walnuts, coconut and cherries. Spread this mixture over the crust and bake in a moderate oven (160°C, 325°F, Gas Mark 3) for about 30 minutes. Cool slightly and cut into squares. Serve warm or cold with whipped cream or ice cream.

Apple Butter Squares

Illustrated opposite
Makes 9

Metric		Imperial
50 g	***Kellogg's Rice Krispies*, finely crushed**	2 oz
200 g	**plain flour**	7 oz
2.5 ml	**salt**	$\frac{1}{2}$ teaspoon
175 g	**butter or margarine**	6 oz
15–30 ml	**milk**	1–2 tablespoons
	Filling	
1.25 ml	**ground cinnamon**	$\frac{1}{4}$ teaspoon
pinch	**grated nutmeg**	pinch
50 g	**sugar**	2 oz
675 g	**cooking apples, peeled, cored and sliced**	$1\frac{1}{2}$ lb
15 ml	**lemon juice**	1 tablespoon
	Icing	
100 g	**icing sugar**	4 oz
15–30 ml	**water**	1–2 tablespoons

Stir together the cereal, flour and salt. Rub in the butter or margarine until the mixture resembles coarse crumbs and add sufficient milk to bind. Roll out half the pastry to cover the base of a 23-cm/9-inch square cake tin. Mix together the filling ingredients and arrange on top. Roll out the remaining pastry to cover the apples and prick with a fork in several places. Bake in a moderately hot oven (190°C, 375°F, Gas Mark 5) for about 45 minutes, until the apples are tender and the pastry golden brown.

Meanwhile mix the icing sugar with enough water to make a smooth consistency. Cut the pastry into squares and drizzle over the icing. Serve warm if liked.

Cherry fritters with cherry sauce (see page 92), Apple butter squares (see above).

Cherry Fritters with Cherry Sauce

Illustrated on page 91
Serves 6

Metric		Imperial
1 (425-g) can	**pitted black cherries**	1 (15-oz) can
225 g	**self-raising flour**	8 oz
5 ml	**salt**	1 teaspoon
50 g	**castor sugar**	2 oz
1	**egg**	1
150 ml	**milk**	$\frac{1}{4}$ pint
10 ml	**vegetable oil**	2 teaspoons
40 g	***Kellogg's All-Bran* or Bran Buds**	$1\frac{1}{2}$ oz
	vegetable oil to deep fry	
15 ml	**cornflour**	1 tablespoon

Drain the cherries, reserving the syrup. Chop half the cherries and keep the remainder for the sauce. Mix together the flour, salt and sugar. In a mixing bowl, beat the egg with the milk and oil. Add the *All-Bran* and allow to stand for a few minutes until the cereal is softened. Stir in the flour mixture, mix until smooth then fold in the chopped cherries.

Heat the oil in a deep fryer to 190°C/375°F. Drop dessertspoonfuls of the cherry batter into the hot oil and fry until deep golden brown all over, about $2\frac{1}{2}$ minutes. Drain on kitchen paper and keep warm while cooking the remainder.

For the sauce, make the reserved cherry syrup up to 300 ml/$\frac{1}{2}$ pint with water. Put the cornflour into a small saucepan and gradually stir in the cherry syrup. Bring to the boil, stirring constantly, and cook for a minute. Stir in the whole cherries and serve warm with the fritters.

Danish Blackcurrant Tartlets

Makes about 18

Metric		Imperial
275 g	**plain flour**	10 oz
5 ml	**salt**	1 teaspoon
175 g	**margarine**	6 oz
45 ml	**boiling water**	3 tablespoons
15 ml	**milk**	1 tablespoon
	Filling	
30 ml	**arrowroot**	2 tablespoons
450 ml	**water**	$\frac{3}{4}$ pint
1 packet	***Kellogg's Rise & Shine Blackcurrant***	1 packet
450 g	**blackcurrants, topped and tailed**	1 lb
225 g	**cream cheese**	8 oz
40 g	**castor sugar**	$1\frac{1}{2}$ oz
1.25 ml	**vanilla essence**	$\frac{1}{4}$ teaspoon

Sift the flour and salt together. Put the margarine, water and milk into a small bowl and, using an electric mixer, beat on medium speed until smooth and thick and the mixture stands in soft peaks. Add the flour and stir quickly with a fork until the dough clings together. Work the dough into a ball, knead lightly until smooth and divide into four. On a floured surface, roll out each piece to about 3 mm/$\frac{1}{8}$ inch thick. Using a 10-cm/ 4-inch pastry cutter, cut out four or five rounds from each piece of pastry. Fit these pastry rounds over the backs of deep bun tins, pinching each into five or six pleats. Prick each tartlet case several times with a fork and bake in a hot oven (230°C, 450°F, Gas Mark 8) for about 7 minutes, until lightly browned. Cool slightly, then carefully remove the pastry cases from the bun tins and cool completely on a wire rack.

Blend the arrowroot with 30 ml/2 tablespoons of the water. Put the remaining water into a saucepan with the *Rise & Shine* and mix well. Add the blackcurrants and bring to the boil. Simmer for 1–2 minutes, until the blackcurrants are beginning to soften, then pour on to the blended arrowroot, stirring. Return to the pan, bring to the boil, stirring, and cook for a minute. Remove from the heat and leave until cold.

Beat the cream cheese, sugar and vanilla essence until light and fluffy. Gently spread over the base and sides of the tartlet cases and spoon a little blackcurrant mixture into each. Chill for 3–4 hours before serving.

Baking

Cereal products make the perfect basis for a whole range of home-baked items. Cookies and biscuits are delicious with a cup of coffee, and favourites with children too. Batch baking is a good idea for those with hungry families, or large freezers – simply double or treble the quantities you make.
You don't have to go to the patisserie to buy appetising breads, cakes and buns; with the help of the easy-to-follow recipes in this section you can have the satisfaction of making them yourself – at home.

Treacle Bread

Illustrated opposite
Makes 1 loaf

Metric		Imperial
150 g	**self-raising flour**	5 oz
5 ml	**baking powder**	1 teaspoon
2.5 ml	**salt**	$\frac{1}{2}$ teaspoon
2.5 ml	**ground cinnamon**	$\frac{1}{2}$ teaspoon
1	**egg**	1
75 g	***Kellogg's All-Bran or Bran Buds***	3 oz
75 g	**seedless raisins**	3 oz
25 g	**lard**	1 oz
60 ml	**treacle**	4 tablespoons
225 ml	**very hot water**	8 fl oz

Sift together the dry ingredients. In a large bowl beat the egg. Mix in the *All-Bran*, seedless raisins, lard and treacle. Add the water, stirring to melt the fat. Fold in the flour and turn into a greased 1-kg/2-lb loaf tin. Bake in a moderate oven (180°C, 350°F, Gas Mark 4) for 45 minutes. Remove from the tin and cool slightly. Serve warm or cool completely, wrap in foil, and serve the following day.

Treacle bread (see above), Bacon bread (see page 96), Three-way yeast bread rolls (see page 97).

Bacon Bread

Illustrated on page 95
Serves 12

Metric		Imperial
350 g	**streaky bacon**	12 oz
100 g	***Kellogg's Corn Flakes*, finely crushed**	4 oz
175 g	**plain flour**	6 oz
15 ml	**baking powder**	1 tablespoon
5 ml	**salt**	1 teaspoon
40 g	**castor sugar**	1$\frac{1}{2}$ oz
	vegetable oil	
2	**eggs, lightly beaten**	2
240 ml	**milk**	8 fl oz

Fry the bacon in its own fat until crisp. Drain on kitchen paper, reserving the dripping, and chop. Put the crushed *Corn Flakes*, flour, baking powder, salt and sugar into a large mixing bowl and stir well. Pour the bacon dripping into a measuring jug and add enough oil to make up to 125 ml/4 fl oz. Stir in the eggs and milk, then add to the *Corn Flakes* mixture, stirring only until combined. Fold in half the chopped bacon. Turn into a greased 20-cm/8-inch square cake tin, spread level and sprinkle the remaining bacon on top.

Bake in a moderately hot oven (200°C, 400°F, Gas Mark 6) for about 30 minutes, or until golden brown and a knife inserted into the centre comes out clean. While still warm, loosen the edges and cut the bread into squares. Serve warm.

To freeze, pack in polythene bags or rigid containers when cold, and freeze quickly. To serve, unwrap and allow to thaw at room temperature for 1–2 hours. To serve warm, thaw and then reheat in a moderate oven (180°C, 350°F, Gas Mark 4) for 5–10 minutes.

Three-Way Yeast Bread Rolls

Illustrated on page 95
Makes 12

Metric		Imperial
7.5 ml	**dried yeast**	$1\frac{1}{2}$ teaspoons
45 ml	**warm water**	3 tablespoons
75 g	**margarine or lard**	3 oz
100 g	***Kellogg's All-Bran or Bran Buds***	4 oz
5 ml	**salt**	1 teaspoon
75 g	**sugar**	3 oz
150 ml	**boiling water**	$\frac{1}{4}$ pint
1	**egg**	1
450 g	**plain flour**	1 lb
15 g	**butter or margarine, melted**	$\frac{1}{2}$ oz

poppy seeds or sesame seeds to sprinkle

Dissolve the yeast in the warm water (this should be hand hot). Put the margarine or lard, *All-Bran*, salt and sugar into a large mixing bowl. Pour over the boiling water and stir until the fat melts. Leave to cool. Stir in the egg and the yeast mixture. Add half the flour, mix well, then add the remaining flour. Stir to combine. Place in a greased bowl, cover and leave to rise until doubled in size (about 1 hour).

Shape the dough into 12 balls. Place on a greased baking tray, cover and leave to rise again until doubled in size. Brush the tops with melted butter, sprinkle with poppy seeds and bake in a moderately hot oven (190°C, 375°F, Gas Mark 5) for about 15 minutes, until lightly browned. Serve warm.

Bran Fruit Loaf

Illustrated opposite
Makes 1 loaf

Metric		Imperial
100 g	**Kellogg's All-Bran or Bran Buds**	4 oz
150 g	**castor sugar**	5 oz
275 g	**mixed dried fruit**	10 oz
300 ml	**milk**	$\frac{1}{2}$ pint
100 g	**self-raising flour**	4 oz

Put the *All-Bran*, sugar and dried fruit into a bowl and mix well together. Stir in the milk and leave to stand for 30 minutes. Sift in the flour, mixing well, and pour the mixture into a well greased 1-kg/2-lb loaf tin. Bake in a moderate oven (180°C, 350°F, Gas Mark 4) for about 1 hour. Turn out of the tin and allow to cool. Cut into slices and, if liked, spread with butter.

Macaroons

Illustrated on page 111
Makes about 18

Metric		Imperial
2	**egg whites**	2
1.25 ml	**cream of tartar**	$\frac{1}{4}$ teaspoon
2.5 ml	**vanilla essence**	$\frac{1}{2}$ teaspoon
150 g	**castor sugar**	5 oz
50 g	**shelled walnuts or pecan nuts, chopped**	2 oz
40 g	**desiccated coconut**	$1\frac{1}{2}$ oz
25 g	**Kellogg's Corn Flakes**	1 oz

Whisk the egg whites until stiff but not dry. Stir in the cream of tartar and vanilla. Gradually add the sugar, whisking until stiff and glossy. Fold in the nuts, coconut and *Corn Flakes*. Drop rounded measuring tablespoonfuls of the mixture on to well greased baking trays and bake in a moderate oven (160°C, 325°F, Gas Mark 3) for 15–20 minutes. Remove immediately and cool on a wire rack.

Delicious cinnamon twists (see page 100), Bran fruit loaf (see above).

Delicious Cinnamon Twists

Illustrated on page 99
Makes 16

Metric		Imperial
40 g	**castor sugar**	$1\frac{1}{2}$ oz
45 ml	**warm water (37°C/100°F)**	3 tablespoons
15 g	**dried yeast**	$\frac{1}{2}$ oz
75 g	**margarine**	3 oz
5 ml	**salt**	1 teaspoon
5 ml	**vanilla essence**	1 teaspoon
90 ml	**milk**	6 tablespoons
500 g	**plain flour**	1 lb 2 oz
3	**eggs, lightly beaten**	3
	Coating	
50 g	***Kellogg's Frosties*, finely crushed**	2 oz
40 g	**almonds, blanched and finely chopped**	$1\frac{1}{2}$ oz
50 g	**castor sugar**	2 oz
5 ml	**ground cinnamon**	1 teaspoon
50 g	**butter or margarine, melted**	2 oz

Put 5 ml/1 teaspoon of the sugar into a jug with the warm water and stir until the sugar has dissolved. Stir in the yeast and leave until frothy. Put the margarine, salt, vanilla essence and remaining sugar into a large mixing bowl. Heat the milk until almost boiling and pour into the bowl. Stir until the fat has melted. Leave until lukewarm then stir in the yeast mixture. Add half the flour, beating until smooth. Gradually add the eggs, beating well after each addition. Add the remaining flour and mix well to form a soft but not sticky dough. Cover lightly and leave in a warm place until doubled in size, about 30 minutes.

Meanwhile, prepare the coating. Mix together the *Frosties*, almonds, sugar and cinnamon. Place in a shallow dish. When the dough has risen, turn on to a lightly floured surface and knead gently. Divide into 16 pieces. Using the fingers, gently roll each to a stick 15 cm/6 inches long. Roll in the melted butter then coat with the *Frosties* mixture, twisting each stick slightly. Place on a baking tray and bake in a moderately hot oven (190°C, 375°F, Gas Mark 5) for about 15 minutes, or until lightly browned. Cool on a wire rack.

To freeze, pack in polythene bags and freeze quickly. To serve, allow to thaw at room temperature, still in the bags, for 1–2 hours.

Wholewheat Bran Bread

Illustrated on the jacket
Makes 1 loaf

Metric		Imperial
175 g	**plain flour**	6 oz
175 g	**wholewheat flour**	6 oz
100 g	***Kellogg's All-Bran* or *Bran Buds***	4 oz
15 ml	**sugar**	1 tablespoon
5 ml	**salt**	1 teaspoon
15 ml	**dried yeast**	1 tablespoon
150 ml	**milk**	$\frac{1}{4}$ pint
15 ml	**treacle**	1 tablespoon
25 g	**butter or margarine**	1 oz
1	**egg**	1
	Decoration	
100 g	**icing sugar**	4 oz
50 g	**glacé cherries, chopped**	2 oz

In a small mixing bowl stir the flours together. Mix one-quarter of the flour with the *All-Bran*, sugar, salt and yeast. In a small saucepan combine the milk, treacle and butter. Place over a low heat until very warm. Gradually add to the *All-Bran* mixture and beat at medium speed with an electric mixer for 2 minutes. Add the egg and sufficient of the flour to make a stiff dough.

On a lightly floured surface, knead the dough for 5 minutes. Place in a greased bowl, cover and leave to rise until doubled in size (about 1–1½ hours). Knock back the dough, then roll into three strips, each about 60 cm/24 inches long. Plait the strips together, then shape into a ring. Place on a greased baking tray, cover and leave to rise in a warm place until doubled in size. Bake in a moderately hot oven (190°C, 375°F, Gas Mark 5) for 20–25 minutes. Cool on a wire rack.

Mix the icing sugar with a little cold water to a thick coating consistency, trickle over the bread and top with the glacé cherries.

Cranberry-Filled Slice

Serves 8–10

Metric		Imperial
1 (397-g) jar	**cranberries in syrup**	1 (14-oz) jar
50 g	**castor sugar**	2 oz
150 ml	**milk and water, warmed to 37°C/100°F**	$\frac{1}{4}$ pint
10 ml	**dried yeast**	2 teaspoons
40 g	***Kellogg's Corn Flakes*, finely crushed**	$1\frac{1}{2}$ oz
2.5 ml	**salt**	$\frac{1}{2}$ teaspoon
325 g	**plain flour**	11 oz
40 g	**margarine**	$1\frac{1}{2}$ oz
1	**egg, lightly beaten**	1
	Decoration	
100 g	**icing sugar, sifted**	4 oz
30 ml	**finely chopped nuts (optional)**	2 tablespoons

Drain off the cranberry syrup and reserve. Dissolve 5 ml/1 teaspoon of the sugar in the milk and water, and stir in the dried yeast. Leave until the yeast is frothy.

Put the *Corn Flakes*, salt, remaining sugar and half the flour into a large mixing bowl. Mix well then rub in the margarine. Add the yeast mixture and the egg. Beat well, then add the remaining flour to make a soft but not sticky dough. On a lightly floured surface, knead the dough until smooth and elastic, about 10 minutes. Place in a greased bowl, cover with cling film and leave to rise in a warm place until doubled in size, about 1 hour.

Turn the dough on to a lightly floured surface, knead lightly, then roll out to a 30 × 23-cm/12 × 9-inch rectangle. Spread the drained cranberries lengthways over half the dough. Fold the other half of the dough over the filling, pressing the edges well together. Place on a greased baking tray. Cover with greased cling film and leave to rise in a warm place until doubled in size, about 30 minutes. Remove the cling film and bake in a moderate oven (180°C, 350°F, Gas Mark 4) for about 20 minutes, until golden brown. Cool on a wire rack.

Mix the icing sugar with a little cold water to a coating consistency and trickle the icing over the cake. Sprinkle with chopped nuts if liked.

Date-Filled Tea Ring

Serves 12

Metric		Imperial
225 g	**stoned dates, chopped**	8 oz
150 ml	**water**	$\frac{1}{4}$ pint
100 g	**castor sugar**	4 oz
60 ml	**warm water (37°C/100°F)**	4 tablespoons
10 ml	**dried yeast**	2 teaspoons
50 g	**margarine**	2 oz
40 g	***Kellogg's All-Bran or Bran Buds***	$1\frac{1}{2}$ oz
2.5 ml	**salt**	$\frac{1}{2}$ teaspoon
60 ml	**boiling water**	4 tablespoons
1	**egg, lightly beaten**	1
275 g	**plain flour**	10 oz
25 g	**butter or margarine, melted**	1 oz
	Decoration	
100 g	**icing sugar, sifted**	4 oz

Put the dates, water and half the sugar into a small saucepan. Cook over a low heat, stirring occasionally, until smooth and thick. Cool.

Dissolve 5 ml/1 teaspoon of the remaining sugar in the warm water. Stir in the yeast and leave until frothy. Put the rest of the sugar into a large mixing bowl with the margarine, *All-Bran* and salt. Add the boiling water and stir until the fat has melted and the *All-Bran* is softened. Leave until lukewarm then stir in the yeast mixture and the egg. Add half the flour and mix well, then add the remaining flour to form a soft but not sticky dough. Place in a greased bowl, turning the dough once to grease the top. Cover and leave in a warm place until doubled in size, about 1 hour. Turn on to a lightly floured surface, knead lightly, then roll out to a 45 × 15-cm/18 × 6-inch rectangle. Brush with melted butter and spread the date mixture evenly over the dough. Roll up like a Swiss roll, starting from long side, and seal the edge. Place the roll on a greased baking tray, shaping it into a ring and pressing the two ends together. With scissors, cut from the outside edge towards the centre at 2.5-cm/1-inch intervals. Twist each section slightly so the cut edge is facing up. Cover lightly and leave in a warm place until doubled in size, about 1 hour. Bake in a moderately hot oven (190°C, 375°F, Gas Mark 5) for 20–25 minutes. Cool on a wire rack.

Mix the icing sugar with enough cold water to give a coating consistency and trickle over the ring. Sprinkle with chopped glacé cherries if liked.

Sweet Chocolate Cake

Metric		Imperial
60 ml	**water**	4 tablespoons
50 g	**plain chocolate**	2 oz
150 g	**plain flour**	5 oz
2.5 ml	**bicarbonate of soda**	$\frac{1}{2}$ teaspoon
1.25 ml	**salt**	$\frac{1}{4}$ teaspoon
50 g	***Kellogg's All-Bran* or *Bran Buds***	2 oz
125 g	**butter or margarine**	4 oz
225 g	**castor sugar**	8 oz
2	**eggs, separated**	2
2.5 ml	**vanilla essence**	$\frac{1}{2}$ teaspoon
75 ml	**buttermilk or yogurt**	5 tablespoons
	Coconut Pecan Frosting	
75 ml	**evaporated milk**	5 tablespoons
100 g	**castor sugar**	4 oz
2	**egg yolks**	2
50 g	**butter**	2 oz
2.5 ml	**vanilla essence**	$\frac{1}{2}$ teaspoon
50 g	**desiccated coconut**	2 oz
50 g	**pecan nuts, chopped**	2 oz

Put the water and chocolate into a saucepan over gentle heat until the chocolate melts. Cool. Stir together the flour, soda, salt and *All-Bran*. Beat the butter with the sugar until pale and fluffy. Add the egg yolks one at a time, beating well after each addition, then beat in the melted chocolate and vanilla essence. Fold in the flour mixture and buttermilk alternately. Whisk the egg whites into soft peaks and fold in.

Turn the mixture into two greased and floured 20-cm/8-inch sandwich tins and bake in a moderate oven (180°C, 350°F, Gas Mark 4) for about 35 minutes, until firm to the touch. Cool completely then remove from the tins.

Combine together all the ingredients for the frosting in a pan. Cook over a gentle heat, stirring frequently, until sufficiently thick to spread. Sandwich the cake layers together and top with the frosting.

Fruit Cake with a Difference

Illustrated on page 107

Metric		Imperial
450 g	mincemeat	1 lb
350 g	mixed dried fruit	12 oz
50 g	chopped mixed peel	2 oz
100 g	glacé cherries, halved	4 oz
100 g	shelled walnuts, chopped	4 oz
225 g	*Kellogg's Corn Flakes*, crushed	8 oz
3	eggs, beaten	3
1 (397-g) can	sweetened condensed milk	1 (14-oz) can
5 ml	ground mixed spice	1 teaspoon
5 ml	baking powder	1 teaspoon

Put all the ingredients into a large bowl and mix thoroughly. Turn the mixture into a greased and lined 20-cm/8-inch round cake tin, and spread level. Bake in a cool oven (150°C, 300°F, Gas Mark 2) for $1\frac{3}{4}$–2 hours, or until a skewer inserted into centre of the cake comes out clean. Allow to cool for 10 minutes in the tin, then turn out and cool on a wire rack.

Chocolate Coconut Chews

Makes 16

Metric		Imperial
100 g	*Kellogg's Corn Flakes*, crushed	4 oz
45 ml	castor sugar	3 tablespoons
75 g	butter, softened	3 oz
125 g	shelled walnuts, coarsely chopped	$4\frac{1}{2}$ oz
125 g	chocolate dots	$4\frac{1}{2}$ oz
100 g	shredded or desiccated coconut	4 oz
1 (397-g) can	sweetened condensed milk	1 (14-oz) can

Put the *Corn Flakes*, sugar and butter into a bowl and mix well together. Press the mixture over the base of an 18 × 28-cm/7 × 11-inch Swiss roll tin and press down firmly with the back of a spoon. Sprinkle with the walnuts, chocolate dots and coconut, and pour the condensed milk evenly over the top. Bake in a moderate oven (180°C, 350°F, Gas Mark 4) for 25 minutes. Cool completely before cutting into squares.

Fresh Apple Cake

Illustrated opposite
Serves 9–12

Metric		Imperial
175 g	**self-raising flour**	6 oz
pinch	**salt**	pinch
2.5 ml	**ground cinnamon**	$\frac{1}{2}$ teaspoon
2.5 ml	**grated nutmeg**	$\frac{1}{2}$ teaspoon
450 g	**cooking apples**	1 lb
125 g	**butter or margarine**	4 oz
175 g	**castor sugar**	6 oz
2	**eggs**	2
50 g	***Kellogg's All-Bran* or *Bran Buds***	2 oz
	Fluffy Icing	
15 ml	**plain flour**	1 tablespoon
45 ml	**milk**	3 tablespoons
50 g	**butter**	2 oz
50 g	**castor sugar**	2 oz

Sift together the flour, salt, cinnamon and nutmeg. Peel, core and finely chop the apples. Beat the butter and sugar together until light and fluffy. Beat in the eggs one at a time, then fold in the flour, apples and *All-Bran*. Turn into a greased and base-lined 23-cm/9-inch square cake tin and spread level. Bake in a moderate oven (180°C, 350°F, Gas Mark 4) for 45 minutes–1 hour, or until the cake is golden brown and shrinking away from the sides of the tin. Turn on to a wire rack and leave until cold.

To make the icing, put the flour into a small saucepan and gradually stir in the milk. Cook over a low heat, stirring constantly, until a thick paste forms. Remove from the heat and leave until cold. Beat the butter with the sugar until light and fluffy. Add the cooled flour paste and beat thoroughly until light and of a spreading consistency. Spread over the apple cake and serve cut into squares.

To freeze, place the cake on a baking tray and open freeze until firm. Wrap in freezer film or a polythene bag, seal and return to the freezer. To serve, unwrap while still frozen and allow to thaw at room temperature for about 3 hours.

Fresh apple cake (see above), Fruit cake with a difference (see page 105).

Chocolate Banana Bars

Illustrated on page 111
Makes 20

Metric		Imperial
175 g	**plain chocolate**	6 oz
50 g	**butter or margarine**	2 oz
100 g	**castor sugar**	4 oz
3	**bananas, mashed**	3
60 ml	**milk**	4 tablespoons
1	**egg**	1
50 g	***Kellogg's All-Bran* or *Bran Buds***	2 oz
175 g	**self-raising flour**	6 oz
5 ml	**salt**	1 teaspoon
2.5 ml	**ground cinnamon**	$\frac{1}{2}$ teaspoon
	Velvet Icing	
175 g	**plain chocolate**	6 oz
25 g	**butter or margarine**	1 oz
60 ml	**milk**	4 tablespoons
2.5 ml	**vanilla essence**	$\frac{1}{2}$ teaspoon
pinch	**salt**	pinch
150 g	**icing sugar, sifted**	5 oz

Melt the chocolate in a basin over a pan of hot water. Cream the butter and sugar together. Add the bananas, milk and egg, and mix well. Stir in the chocolate, *All-Bran*, flour, salt and cinnamon and beat until well blended. Spread the mixture in a greased and base-lined Swiss roll tin, 18 × 28 × 3 cm/7 × 11 × 1¼ inches. Bake in a moderate oven (180°C, 350°F, Gas Mark 4) for about 30 minutes then turn out and leave until cold.

To make the icing, melt the chocolate and butter in a basin over a pan of hot water. Remove from the heat. Add the milk, vanilla essence, salt and icing sugar and beat until smooth. Leave until a thick coating consistency forms, stirring occasionally. Spread over the chocolate cake and when the icing has set, cut into 20 bars.

To freeze, open freeze until firm, then pack in rigid containers or polythene bags and store until required. To serve, unwrap and allow to thaw at room temperature for about 2 hours.

Raisin Bars

Illustrated on page 111
Makes 20

Metric		Imperial
100 g	**butter or margarine**	4 oz
100 g	**granulated sugar**	4 oz
100 g	**light soft brown sugar**	4 oz
2	**eggs**	2
5 ml	**vanilla essence**	1 teaspoon
40 g	***Kellogg's All-Bran* or *Bran Buds***	$1\frac{1}{2}$ oz
100 g	**self-raising flour**	4 oz
2.5 ml	**salt**	$\frac{1}{2}$ teaspoon
100 g	**seedless raisins**	4 oz
	Icing	
200 g	**icing sugar**	7 oz
25 g	**butter or margarine, softened**	1 oz
15 ml	**milk**	1 tablespoon
2.5 ml	**vanilla essence**	$\frac{1}{2}$ teaspoon

Beat the butter and sugars together until light and creamy. Beat in the eggs, one at a time, then add the vanilla essence. Fold in the *All-Bran*. Sift the flour with the salt and fold into the cake mixture with the raisins. Turn into a greased and base-lined Swiss roll tin, $18 \times 28 \times 3$ cm/$7 \times 11 \times 1\frac{1}{4}$ inches. Bake in a moderate oven (180°C, 350°F, Gas Mark 4) for about 30 minutes, until well risen and golden brown. Turn out and cool on a wire rack.

To make the icing, put all the ingredients into a mixing bowl and beat until smooth. Spread over the cooled cake then cut into 20 bars.

To freeze, place the bars on a baking tray and open freeze until firm, then pack in foil, freezer film or rigid containers and return to the freezer. To serve, unwrap and allow to thaw at room temperature for 1–2 hours.

Cherry Winks

Illustrated opposite
Makes about 18

Metric		Imperial
100 g	**self-raising flour**	4 oz
1.25 ml	**bicarbonate of soda**	$\frac{1}{4}$ teaspoon
50 g	**butter or margarine**	2 oz
50 g	**castor sugar**	2 oz
1	**egg**	1
2.5 ml	**vanilla essence**	$\frac{1}{2}$ teaspoon
50 g	**almonds, blanched and chopped**	2 oz
50 g	**glacé cherries, chopped**	2 oz
50 g	**stoned dates, chopped**	2 oz
15 ml	**milk**	1 tablespoon
50 g	***Kellogg's Corn Flakes*, finely crushed**	2 oz
	quartered glacé cherries to decorate	

Sift the flour and soda together. Beat the butter with the sugar until fluffy. Beat in the egg and vanilla. Stir in the flour then add the almonds, cherries, dates and milk and mix well. Shape teaspoons of the mixture into balls and roll in the crushed *Corn Flakes*. Place well apart on greased baking trays and top each with a cherry quarter. Bake in a moderate oven (180°C, 350°F, Gas Mark 4) for 15 minutes. Cool on a wire rack.

Chocolate wafer sandwich biscuits (see page 112), Macaroons (see page 98), Chocolate banana bars (see page 108), Raisin bars (see page 109), Cherry winks (see above).

Chocolate Wafer Sandwich Biscuits

Illustrated on page 111
Makes about 20

Metric		Imperial
50 g	***Kellogg's Rice Krispies***	2 oz
100 g	**butter or margarine**	4 oz
225 g	**castor sugar**	8 oz
1	**egg**	1
5 ml	**vanilla essence**	1 teaspoon
50 g	**plain chocolate, melted**	2 oz
175 g	**plain flour**	6 oz
3.75 ml	**salt**	$\frac{3}{4}$ teaspoon
75 g	**shelled walnuts, roughly chopped**	3 oz
	Icing	
200 g	**icing sugar, sifted**	7 oz
25 g	**butter or margarine, softened**	1 oz
15 ml	**milk**	1 tablespoon
2.5 ml	**vanilla essence**	$\frac{1}{2}$ teaspoon

Lightly crush the *Rice Krispies* to half their previous volume. In a large mixing bowl, beat together the butter and sugar until light and fluffy. Add the egg, vanilla essence and melted chocolate, beating well. Sift in the flour and salt and mix well. Add the *Rice Krispies* and walnuts and mix until combined. Place rounded measuring teaspoonfuls of the mixture on to lightly greased baking trays, allowing a little room for spreading. Flatten slightly with the palm of the hand and bake in a moderate oven (160°C, 325°F, Gas Mark 3) for about 10 minutes, until set. Leave on the trays for a few minutes then transfer to a wire cooling rack and leave until cold.

To make the icing, place all the ingredients in a mixing bowl and beat until smooth. Sandwich the biscuits in pairs with a little icing, and spread a little more on top of each. If liked, sprinkle the icing with chopped walnuts.

Cooking for Children

When children's parties present a problem, and varied and exciting dishes must be created, the following section may help you. Both sweet and savoury recipes are included which will appeal to children of all ages. A tiger in the form of a birthday cake can delight many a child and highlight the party spread, while there's even a Footballer's Cake for the enthusiastic young sportsman. Moving away from the party scene the supper dishes here are quick, easy to make and full of cereal goodness – sure to be favourites among children. Some of the recipes in this section are easy enough for children to make themselves. Allowing the children to cook can be an excellent way to keep them quiet for an hour or two, under your eye in the kitchen; not only will it keep them occupied but it will teach them the basic elements of cooking.

Dotty Cookies

Makes about 60

Metric		Imperial
250 g	**plain flour**	9 oz
2.5 ml	**bicarbonate of soda**	$\frac{1}{2}$ teaspoon
2.5 ml	**salt**	$\frac{1}{2}$ teaspoon
225 g	**butter or margarine**	8 oz
225 g	**castor sugar**	8 oz
2	**eggs**	2
5 ml	**vanilla essence**	1 teaspoon
40 g	***Kellogg's Frosties*, crushed**	$1\frac{1}{2}$ oz
175 g	**chocolate dots, melted**	6 oz

Stir together the flour, soda and salt. In a large mixing bowl beat the butter with the sugar until pale and fluffy. Beat in the eggs and vanilla essence. Add the flour then stir in the *Frosties*. Drizzle melted chocolate over the mixture and swirl through gently with the point of a knife. Drop tablespoonfuls on to greased baking trays and bake in a moderate oven (180°C, 350°F, Gas Mark 4) for about 12 minutes, until lightly browned. Cool on wire racks.

Celebration Cake

Illustrated opposite

Metric		Imperial
175 g	**butter**	6 oz
175 g	**castor sugar**	6 oz
3	**eggs, beaten**	3
175 g	**self-raising flour**	6 oz
	Filling and Topping	
	raspberry jam	
300 ml	**double cream, whipped**	$\frac{1}{2}$ pint
40 g	***Kellogg's Corn Flakes***	$1\frac{1}{2}$ oz
75 g	**plain chocolate, melted**	3 oz

Cream the butter and sugar until light. Add the eggs gradually, beating well. Fold in the flour and divide between two greased 20-cm/8-inch sandwich tins. Bake at 190°C, 375°F, Gas Mark 5 for 20–25 minutes, then turn out and cool.

Spread raspberry jam on one cake. Spread over half the cream and top with the second cake. Spread the remaining jam and cream on top. Mix the *Corn Flakes* into the cooled melted chocolate and spoon over the top of the cake. Chill for 10–15 minutes.

Fruitie Squares

Illustrated opposite
Makes 12

Metric		Imperial
25 g	**butter**	1 oz
25 g	**sugar**	1 oz
15 ml	**golden syrup**	1 tablespoon
75 g	***Kellogg's Smacks***	3 oz
25 g	**sultanas**	1 oz
15 g	**glacé cherries, chopped**	$\frac{1}{2}$ oz
15 g	**chopped mixed peel**	$\frac{1}{2}$ oz

Melt the butter, add the sugar and syrup and simmer for about 5 minutes, until a light brown colour. Stir in the remaining ingredients and turn into a lightly greased 20-cm/8-inch square tin. When cool cut into 12 squares.

Ice cream delight (see page 116), Fruitie squares, Celebration cake (see above), Cheese snacks (see page 116).

Ice Cream Delight

Illustrated on page 115
Serves 6

Metric		Imperial
25 g	**Kellogg's Rice Krispies**	1 oz
25 g	**desiccated coconut**	1 oz
25 g	**shelled walnuts, chopped**	1 oz
25 g	**soft brown sugar**	1 oz
50 g	**butter, melted**	2 oz
1 (483-ml) block	**strawberry ice cream**	1 (17-fl oz) block
75 g	**plain chocolate, melted**	3 oz

Put the *Rice Krispies*, coconut, walnuts and soft brown sugar into a large bowl. Mix together. Add the melted butter and stir until the *Rice Krispies* are well coated. Press the mixture into a shallow, greased 20-cm/8-inch square tin and chill for 30 minutes. Cut into six rectangles. Cut the ice cream into six 2.5-cm/1-inch thick slices and place a slice on each biscuit. Trickle the melted chocolate in a zig-zag pattern over the ice cream and serve at once.

Cheese Snacks

Illustrated on page 115
Makes about 20

Metric		Imperial
100 g	**plain flour**	4 oz
	salt and pepper	
100 g	**butter**	4 oz
100 g	**cheese, finely grated**	4 oz
1	**egg, separated**	1
25 g	**Kellogg's Rice Krispies**	1 oz

Sift the flour and seasoning into a bowl. Rub in the butter then add the cheese and egg yolk, mixing well together. Knead lightly. Roll out on a lightly floured surface to 5 mm/$\frac{1}{4}$ inch thick and cut into rounds with a 4.5-cm/1$\frac{3}{4}$-inch cutter. Place the rounds on a baking tray. Lightly beat the egg white and brush over each biscuit. Sprinkle *Rice Krispies* on top and bake in a moderately hot oven (200°C, 400°F, Gas Mark 6) for about 20 minutes. Cool on a wire rack.

Rice 'n' Toffee Cake

Serves 8

Metric		Imperial
50 g	**butter or margarine**	2 oz
100 g	**toffees or caramels**	4 oz
25 g	**castor sugar**	1 oz
65 g	***Kellogg's Puffa Puffa Rice***	$2\frac{1}{2}$ oz
	Decoration	
175 g	**icing sugar, sifted**	6 oz
30 ml	**lemon juice**	2 tablespoons
	glacé cherries, halved	
	angelica leaves	

Melt the butter in a saucepan over gentle heat. Add the toffees and stir until melted. Mix in the sugar and *Puffa Puffa Rice* and combine well. Place a greased 18-cm/7-inch flan ring on a greased baking tray and press the toffee mixture into it. Press down well and chill in the refrigerator.

Mix the icing sugar and lemon juice together and spread over the top of the cake. Decorate with halved glacé cherries and angelica.

Toffee Triangles

Makes 18

Metric		Imperial
100 g	**toffees**	4 oz
30 ml	**double cream**	2 tablespoons
65 g	***Kellogg's Ricicles***	$2\frac{1}{2}$ oz

In a small pan, melt the toffees over a gentle heat and stir in the cream. Put the *Ricicles* into a buttered basin. Pour over the toffee mixture and combine well together. Press into a shallow, buttered 18-cm/7-inch square tin and leave until cold. Cut into nine squares then cut each square diagonally to make triangles.

Humpty Dumpty Cake

Illustrated opposite

Metric		Imperial
65 g	***Kellogg's All-Bran or Bran Buds***	$2\frac{1}{2}$ oz
150 ml	**milk**	$\frac{1}{4}$ pint
175 g	**butter or margarine**	6 oz
175 g	**light soft brown sugar**	6 oz
3	**eggs, beaten**	3
175 g	**self-raising flour**	6 oz
100 g	**plain chocolate, melted**	4 oz
	Icing and Decoration	
175 g	**butter or margarine**	6 oz
350 g	**icing sugar, sifted**	12 oz
15 ml	**milk**	1 tablespoon
100 g	**plain chocolate, melted**	4 oz
225 g	**marzipan**	8 oz
	chocolate buttons	

Soften the *All-Bran* with the milk in a bowl. Beat the butter and sugar then gradually beat in the eggs. Fold in the *All-Bran* and flour then stir in the chocolate. Spread half in a greased and base-lined, shallow 18-cm/7-inch square tin and divide the remainder between two greased and floured 0.75-litre/1-pint pudding basins. Place on baking trays and cook in a moderate oven (180°C, 350°F, Gas Mark 4) for 30–40 minutes. Turn out and cool.

Beat the butter until soft. Gradually beat in the icing sugar and milk and reserve 30 ml/2 tablespoons of this icing. Beat the melted chocolate into the remainder. Cut the square cake in half lengthways and sandwich together with chocolate icing. Stand the cake on a board, with the cut edge downwards, and coat with chocolate icing. Pipe a brick pattern on the wall with the plain icing. Use half the marzipan to make arms and legs. Flatten the ends of the legs and place on the top of the wall, so the legs hang over the front. Trim the wide base of each 'egg half' to make a flat surface. Sandwich together with chocolate icing, sealing in the ends of the marzipan arms, as illustrated. Stand the egg on the wall over the flattened part of the legs. Shape the remaining marzipan on top of the egg to form the pointed end and ice the egg all over. Pipe nose, eyes and mouth on to the face and use chocolate buttons to form a belt. Finally top with a party hat.

Humpty Dumpty cake (see above).

Crunchy Ham and Cheese Sandwiches

Serves 2

Metric		Imperial
40 g	**Kellogg's Rice Krispies, finely crushed**	1½ oz
1	**egg**	1
45 ml	**milk**	3 tablespoons
	salt	
2	**slices cheese**	2
2	**thin slices ham**	2
4	**slices day-old bread**	4
25 g	**butter, melted**	1 oz

Put the *Rice Krispies* on to a large plate. In a shallow dish beat the egg and milk with a generous pinch of salt. Make up two sandwiches with one slice each of cheese and ham and two slices of bread. Dip first in the egg, then in the *Rice Krispies*. Place on a greased baking tray, drizzle with the butter and bake in a hot oven (230°C, 450°F, Gas Mark 8) for 10–15 minutes, until crisp and golden.

Date Nut Balls

Makes about 20

Metric		Imperial
50 g	**butter or margarine**	2 oz
175 g	**stoned dates, chopped**	6 oz
50 g	**maraschino cherries, chopped**	2 oz
75 g	**sugar**	3 oz
40 g	**Kellogg's Special K**	1½ oz
100 g	**nuts, chopped**	4 oz

Put the butter, dates, cherries and sugar into a medium pan. Cook over a gentle heat, stirring constantly until the mixture becomes a soft paste. Remove from the heat, stir in the *Special K* and nuts and mix thoroughly. Shape into balls about the size of a walnut and allow to cool.

Chocolate Crackles

Makes about 30

Metric		Imperial
100 g	**plain chocolate**	4 oz
100 g	**butter or margarine**	4 oz
60 ml	**golden syrup**	4 tablespoons
100 g	*Kellogg's Corn Flakes*	4 oz
150 g	**stoned dates, chopped**	5 oz
50 g	**shelled walnuts, chopped**	2 oz

Melt the chocolate in a basin over a pan of hot water. Melt the butter in a pan and add the golden syrup. Heat until just warmed. Combine the remaining ingredients together in a large mixing bowl and add the melted chocolate, butter and syrup. Mix well and allow to firm slightly. Roll spoonfuls of the mixture into balls and place in paper cases. Leave to set.

Crunchy Florentines

Illustrated on the jacket
Makes about 12

Metric		Imperial
50 g	**butter or margarine**	2 oz
15 ml	**honey**	1 tablespoon
50 g	**stoned dates, chopped**	2 oz
50 g	**seedless raisins**	2 oz
50 g	**glacé cherries, chopped**	2 oz
15 ml	**blanched chopped almonds**	1 tablespoon
50 g	*Kellogg's Rice Krispies*	2 oz
	Topping	
175 g	**plain chocolate**	6 oz
30 ml	**milk**	2 tablespoons

Melt the butter with the honey. Add the dates and cook for 1 minute, stirring all the time. Remove from the heat and stir in the raisins, cherries, almonds and *Rice Krispies*. Turn into a shallow, buttered, 18-cm/7-inch square tin and press down firmly.

Place the chocolate and milk in a basin over a pan of hot water and heat gently, stirring frequently until the chocolate has melted. Pour over the florentines and spread evenly. Leave until set. Cut into squares or fingers.

Cuckoo Clock Cake

Illustrated opposite

Metric		Imperial
65 g	***Kellogg's All-Bran* or *Bran Buds***	2½ oz
150 ml	**milk**	¼ pint
175 g	**butter or margarine**	6 oz
175 g	**light soft brown sugar**	6 oz
3	**eggs, beaten**	3
175 g	**self-raising flour**	6 oz
100 g	**plain chocolate, melted**	4 oz
	Icing	
75 g	**butter or margarine**	3 oz
175 g	**icing sugar, sifted**	6 oz
15 ml	**milk**	1 tablespoon
75 g	**plain chocolate, melted**	3 oz
	Decoration	
2 packets	**chocolate finger biscuits**	2 packets
	small model bird	

Put the *All-Bran* and milk into a bowl and leave until the milk is absorbed. Beat the butter with the sugar until light and fluffy. Gradually beat in the eggs, then fold in the *All-Bran* and flour. Gently stir in the melted chocolate. Turn the mixture into a greased and base-lined 18 × 23-cm/7 × 9-inch cake tin. Bake in a moderate oven (180°C, 350°F, Gas Mark 4) for 50 minutes–1 hour, until springy to the touch. Turn out and cool.

When cold, cut two top corners from the cake to make the roof shape, as illustrated, and place the cake on a cake board. To make the icing, beat the butter until soft. Gradually beat in the icing sugar and milk. Reserve 30 ml/2 tablespoons of the plain icing for decoration and add the melted chocolate to the remainder, mixing well. Use the chocolate icing to coat the sides and top of the cake, reserving a little for decoration. Arrange halved chocolate finger biscuits around the sides of the cake to resemble wood. Put the plain icing into a piping bag fitted with a small plain nozzle and pipe a clock face in the centre of the cake (with the small hand pointing to the child's age if the cake is being used as a birthday cake). Pipe doors for the cuckoo above the clock. With the reserved chocolate icing, pipe a little decoration in the corners and around the clock face. Finally place the bird in between the doors and decorate the cake with flowers.

Cuckoo clock cake (see above).

Chocolate Lemon Dominoes

Makes 12

Metric		Imperial
45 ml	**lemon curd**	3 tablespoons
75 g	***Kellogg's Ricicles***	3 oz
175 g	**plain chocolate**	6 oz
10 ml	**lemon curd to decorate**	2 teaspoons

Put the lemon curd into a small pan and bring to the boil, stirring. Boil for 1 minute, allow to cool slightly, then stir in the *Ricicles*. Turn into a shallow, greased 18-cm/7-inch square tin and press down well. Melt the chocolate in a basin over a pan of hot water and spread over the *Ricicles* mixture. Allow to set, then remove from the tin and cut into 12 bars. Put the lemon curd into a piping bag fitted with a small plain nozzle and pipe domino markings on top of each bar.

Chewy Orange Crisps

Makes about 24

Metric		Imperial
150 g	**plain flour**	5 oz
1.25 ml	**bicarbonate of soda**	$\frac{1}{4}$ teaspoon
1.25 ml	**salt**	$\frac{1}{4}$ teaspoon
100 g	**butter or margarine**	4 oz
100 g	**granulated sugar**	4 oz
50 g	**light soft brown sugar**	2 oz
5 ml	**finely grated orange rind**	1 teaspoon
1	**egg**	1
50 g	***Kellogg's Sultana Bran***	2 oz

Sift the flour, bicarbonate of soda and salt together. Beat the butter with the sugars and orange rind until light and creamy. Beat in the egg, add the flour and mix well. Stir in the *Sultana Bran*. Place rounded teaspoonfuls of the mixture on to ungreased baking trays, allowing room for spreading, and bake in a moderate oven (180°C, 350°F, Gas Mark 4) for about 15 minutes, until golden brown. Cool slightly on the trays, then transfer to a wire rack and leave until cold.

Party Cake

Metric		Imperial
175 g	**margarine, softened**	6 oz
175 g	**castor sugar**	6 oz
3	**eggs, beaten**	3
175 g	**self-raising flour**	6 oz
2.5 ml	**grated nutmeg**	$\frac{1}{2}$ teaspoon
2.5 ml	**ground cinnamon**	$\frac{1}{2}$ teaspoon
	Icing and Decoration	
75 g	**margarine, softened**	3 oz
175 g	**icing sugar, sifted**	6 oz
	Kellogg's Frosties	
	chocolate vermicelli	
	2 green and 1 red Smarties	
25 g	**plain chocolate, melted**	1 oz

Cream the margarine with the sugar. Gradually beat in the eggs. Sift the flour with the spices and fold in. Turn into a greased 20-cm/8-inch round cake tin and bake in a moderate oven (180°C, 350°F, Gas Mark 4) for 35–45 minutes. Cool the cake before decorating it to resemble a tiger.

Beat the margarine and icing sugar together until light and fluffy. Mark the cake lightly into four equal segments to give a cross. Arrange the cake so that the cross is at right angles in front of you. At the top edge of the vertical line of the cross, mark 1 cm/$\frac{1}{2}$ inch either side and cut the cake from this mark to the outer edge of the horizontal line of the cross on each side. Cut these ear shapes in half and sandwich together with icing to form ears. Spread all over with icing then coat in *Frosties*. Spread the sides and top of the cake with icing and coat the sides in *Frosties*. Taking the picture on the *Frosties* packet as a guide, lightly mark eyebrows, nose, mouth and stripes in the icing. Sprinkle chocolate vermicelli on the eyebrows and stripes. Arrange *Frosties* around edge of the cake and down the length of the nose. Place green Smarties on the icing for eyes. Pipe chocolate eyelids, pupils, nose tip, mouth and small lines under the mouth. Place the red Smartie on the mouth for a tongue. Pipe a chocolate line on top of the Smartie, then pipe chocolate whiskers either side of the nose. Place the tiger face on a serving plate and put the ears into position. Tie a red bow around the bottom edge of the cake.

Footballer's Cake

Illustrated opposite

Metric		Imperial
65 g	***Kellogg's All-Bran* or *Bran Buds***	$2\frac{1}{2}$ oz
150 ml	**milk**	$\frac{1}{4}$ pint
175 g	**butter or margarine**	6 oz
175 g	**light soft brown sugar**	6 oz
3	**eggs, beaten**	3
175 g	**self-raising flour**	6 oz
100 g	**plain chocolate, melted**	4 oz
	Icing	
75 g	**butter or margarine**	3 oz
175 g	**icing sugar, sifted**	6 oz
15 ml	**milk**	1 tablespoon
75 g	**plain chocolate, melted**	3 oz
	Decoration	
40 g	**desiccated coconut**	$1\frac{1}{2}$ oz
few drops	**green food colouring**	few drops
	small model footballers	
	round chocolate sweet or hazelnut	

Put the *All-Bran* and milk into a bowl and leave until the milk is absorbed. Beat the butter with the sugar then gradually beat in the eggs. Fold in the *All-Bran* and flour, then gently stir in the chocolate. Turn into a greased and base-lined 18 × 23-cm/7 × 9-inch cake tin. Bake in a moderate oven (180°C, 350°F, Gas Mark 4) for 50 minutes–1 hour. Turn out, remove the lining paper and cool.

To make the icing, beat the butter until soft. Gradually beat in the icing sugar and milk. Reserve 30 ml/2 tablespoons for decoration and add the melted chocolate to the remainder. Mix well and use to coat the sides and top of the cake.

Put the coconut into a small bowl, add the green colouring and mix well until the coconut turns green. Press the coconut over the top of the cake. Put the plain icing into a piping bag fitted with a small plain nozzle and pipe football pitch markings over the coconut grass. Use cocktail sticks and scraps of net fabric to make goals and place at each end of the cake. Arrange footballers on the cake and add a round chocolate sweet to represent the ball.

Footballer's cake (see above).

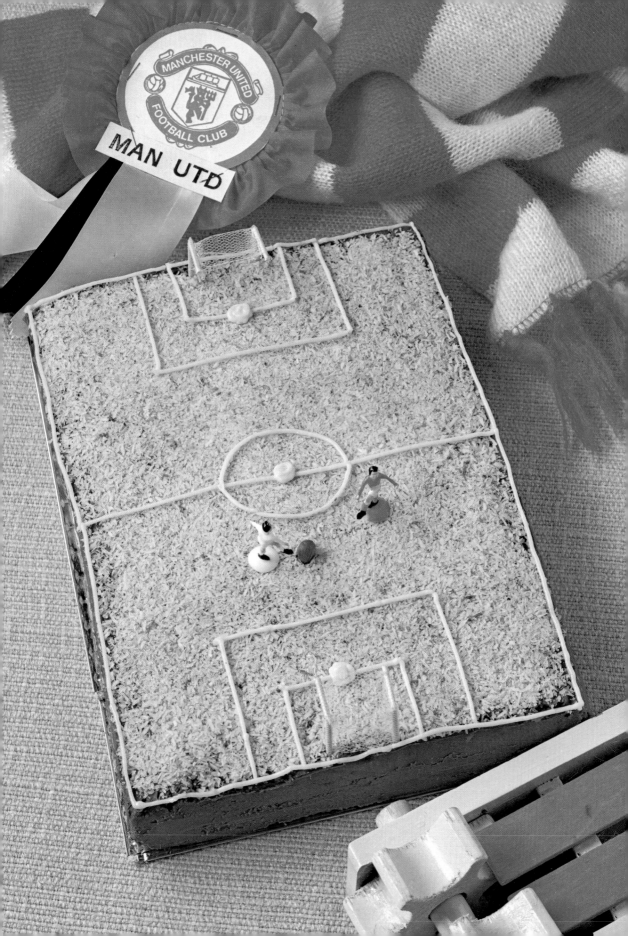

Citrus Ice Lollies

Makes 12

Metric		Imperial
1 packet	**Kellogg's Rise & Shine Lemon**	1 packet
1 packet	**Kellogg's Rise & Shine Orange**	1 packet
600 ml	**cold water**	1 pint

Whisk the ingredients together in a bowl. Pour into 12 ice lolly moulds and freeze on normal setting in the ice compartment of the refrigerator. Leave the moulds in the refrigerator until required.

Ice Cream Party Pie

Serves 8

Metric		Imperial
75 ml	**peanut butter**	5 tablespoons
75 ml	**golden syrup**	5 tablespoons
50 g	**Kellogg's Rice Krispies**	2 oz
90 ml	**jam**	6 tablespoons
1 (1-litre) carton	**ice cream**	1 (35.2-fl oz) carton

Combine the peanut butter and golden syrup until well mixed. Stir in the *Rice Krispies* and coat evenly. Use this mixture to line the base and sides of a 23-cm/9-inch flan tin and chill in the refrigerator.

Spread half the jam over the base of the flan case and pile in the ice cream. Freeze until firm. Swirl the remaining jam over the top of the pie just before serving.

Luscious Apricot Bars

Makes about 18

Metric		Imperial
100 g	**butter or margarine**	4 oz
50 g	**granulated sugar**	2 oz
75 g	**plain flour**	3 oz
25 g	***Kellogg's All-Bran* or *Bran Buds***	1 oz
	Topping	
75 g	**dried apricots, finely chopped**	3 oz
100 g	**light soft brown sugar**	4 oz
2	**eggs**	2
2.5 ml	**vanilla essence**	$\frac{1}{2}$ teaspoon
50 g	**self-raising flour**	2 oz
pinch	**salt**	pinch
50 g	**shelled walnuts, finely chopped**	2 oz
	icing sugar to sprinkle	

Put the butter, granulated sugar and plain flour into a small mixing bowl. Beat until smooth then mix in the *All-Bran*. Spread the mixture evenly over the base of an 18 × 23-cm/7 × 9-inch cake tin. Bake in a moderate oven (180°C, 350°F, Gas Mark 4) for 15–20 minutes, until lightly browned. Remove from the oven and cool slightly.

Meanwhile, put the apricots into a small bowl, cover with very hot water and allow to stand for 10 minutes, until tender. Drain well. Whisk together the brown sugar, eggs and vanilla essence until the mixture is light and retains the impression of the whisk for a few seconds. Sift the flour with the salt and fold into the whisked eggs with the apricots and walnuts. Spread this mixture over the baked crust, return to the oven and bake for a further 40–50 minutes, until well risen and golden brown. Turn out and cool on a wire rack. When cold, sprinkle with icing sugar and cut into bars.

To freeze, do not sprinkle with icing sugar. Wrap in foil, freezer film or polythene bags, seal and freeze. To serve, remove wrapping and allow to thaw at room temperature for about 2 hours, then dust with icing sugar.

Drinks

Drinks of every variety are included in this section, from cocktails to children's fruit drinks, hot winter warmers to refreshing summer coolers.

Hot and cold punches are ideal for parties throughout the year, and especially useful as they can be made in large quantities for any number of guests. An attractive way to serve cold summer drinks is to dip the rim of each glass in a little egg white, followed by white or coloured sugar. Leave the glasses to dry, then pour in the cooled drink. Serve with a slice of fruit placed over the rim of each glass.

Fun recipes for children's parties combine drinks that the children will enjoy with the high vitamin C content found in *Kellogg's Rise & Shine* and *Kellogg's Two Shakes*.

Winter or summer, all these drinks are quick, easy and convenient to make – saving time and giving you the chance to enjoy a long and cool or hot and warming one yourself!

Lemon Balalaika

Illustrated opposite
Serves 4

Metric		Imperial
1 packet	**Kellogg's Rise & Shine Lemon**	1 packet
1	**miniature bottle Cointreau *or* 2 measures**	1
2	**miniature bottles vodka *or* 4 measures**	2
8	**orange slices**	8

Make up the *Rise & Shine* according to packet instructions. Mix together the lemon drink, Cointreau and vodka and shake or whisk well together. Pour over ice into four glasses and serve with orange slices.

Citrus refresher, Icy blackcurrant surprise, Pina colada (see page 132), Lemon Balalaika (see above).

Pina Colada

Illustrated on page 131
Serves 3–4

Metric		Imperial
1 packet	**Kellogg's Rise & Shine Pineapple**	1 packet
3	**miniature bottles white rum *or* 6 measures**	3
60 ml	**cream of coconut**	4 tablespoons

Make up the *Rise & Shine* according to packet instructions. Mix together the rum and cream of coconut and top up with pineapple drink. Shake or blend well and pour over ice into tall glasses. Serve with a straw.

Citrus Refresher

Illustrated on page 131
Serves 16–20

Metric		Imperial
2 packets	**Kellogg's Rise & Shine Grapefruit**	2 packets
2 packets	**Kellogg's Rise & Shine Lemon**	2 packets
1.75 litres	**water**	3 pints
1.15 litres	**cold tea**	2 pints
3	**bananas, thinly sliced**	3

Blend the Grapefruit and Lemon *Rise & Shine* with the water. Stir in the cold tea and chill well. Just before serving, stir in the sliced bananas.

Icy Blackcurrant Surprise

Illustrated on page 131
Serves 2–4

Metric		Imperial
1 packet	**Kellogg's Rise & Shine Blackcurrant**	1 packet
600 ml	**lemonade**	1 pint
1	**individual block vanilla ice cream**	1

Put all ingredients into a large jug and whisk together until thoroughly blended. Pour into tall glasses to serve.

Orange Quencher

Illustrated on the jacket
Serves 3

Metric		Imperial
1 packet	***Kellogg's Rise & Shine* Orange**	1 packet
1	**egg white**	1
30 ml	**sherry**	2 tablespoons
	fresh orange segments	
	cocktail cherries (optional)	

Make up the *Rise & Shine* according to packet instructions. Add the egg white and sherry and beat with an electric mixer or hand whisk until frothy. Serve with fresh orange segments and cocktail cherries.

St. Clement's Sparkle

Illustrated on the jacket
Serves 8–10

Metric		Imperial
1 packet	***Kellogg's Rise & Shine* Orange**	1 packet
1 packet	***Kellogg's Rise & Shine* Lemon**	1 packet
1.4 litres	**lemonade**	$2\frac{1}{2}$ pints
1	**orange, sliced**	1

Put the *Rise & Shine* into a large jug or bowl and add the lemonade, stirring. Float orange slices on top or place over the rim of each glass, and add ice cubes if liked. Serve immediately.

Spicy Hot Tea Punch

Illustrated opposite
Serves 8–10

Metric		Imperial
1.15 litres	**water**	2 pints
300 ml	***Kellogg's Rise & Shine* Orange** (**made up**)	$\frac{1}{2}$ pint
150 ml	***Kellogg's Rise & Shine* Lemon** (**made up**)	$\frac{1}{4}$ pint
100 g	**castor sugar**	4 oz
10 ml	**whole cloves**	2 teaspoons
1	**cinnamon stick**	1
5 ml	**whole allspice**	1 teaspoon
2	**tea bags**	2

Put all the ingredients except the tea bags into a large saucepan and bring to the boil. Reduce the heat and simmer for 5 minutes. Remove from the heat, add the tea bags and allow to infuse for 5 minutes. Discard the tea bags and spices and serve hot.

Orange Fruit Punch

Illustrated opposite
Serves 16

Metric		Imperial
2 packets	***Kellogg's Rise & Shine* Orange**	2 packets
1.75 litres	**water**	3 pints
600 ml	**lime cordial**	1 pint
225 g	**grapes, halved and pipped**	8 oz
1 (411-g) can	**peaches, drained and chopped**	1 (14$\frac{1}{2}$-oz) can

Blend the *Rise & Shine* with the water and lime cordial in a large saucepan. Heat through slowly for about 15 minutes. Add the grapes and peaches and serve hot.

Witches' brew (see page 136), Spicy hot tea punch, Orange fruit punch (see above).

Witches' Brew

Illustrated on page 135
Serves 4

Metric		Imperial
1 packet	**Kellogg's Rise & Shine Blackcurrant**	1 packet
1	**miniature bottle dark rum *or* 2 measures**	1
1	**lemon, sliced**	1

Make up the *Rise & Shine* with water as directed on the packet. Put all ingredients into a saucepan and heat until steaming. Serve hot.

Caribbean Combo

Illustrated on page 139
Serves 4

Metric		Imperial
100 g	**grapes, pipped**	4 oz
2	**oranges, segmented**	2
1 (40-g) packet	**Kellogg's Two Shakes Banana Flavour**	1 (1.4-oz) packet
568 ml	**cold milk**	1 pint
4	**orange slices**	4

Place half the grapes, the oranges, Banana *Two Shakes* and milk into a blender for 30 seconds. Strain. Chop the remaining grapes finely and stir into the banana mixture. Pour into glasses and place an orange slice over the rim of each glass.

Banana Foam

Illustrated on page 139
Serves 4

Metric		Imperial
1 (40-g) packet	**Kellogg's Two Shakes Banana Flavour**	1 (1.4-oz) packet
50 g	**dried figs, soaked overnight**	2 oz
2.5 ml	**grated nutmeg**	$\frac{1}{2}$ teaspoon
568 ml	**cold milk**	1 pint
	crushed macaroons to sprinkle	

Whizz the Banana *Two Shakes*, figs, nutmeg and milk in a blender for 30 seconds. Strain, then pour into mugs and sprinkle crushed macaroons on the top.

Chocolate Icebreaker

Illustrated on page 139
Serves 4

Metric		Imperial
1 (40-g) packet	**Kellogg's Two Shakes Chocolate Flavour**	1 (1.4-oz) packet
300 ml	**milk**	$\frac{1}{2}$ pint
300 ml	**ginger ale**	$\frac{1}{2}$ pint
	crushed ice	
	double cream	

Mix the Chocolate *Two Shakes*, milk and ginger ale together. Place crushed ice in the bottom of four mugs, pour the chocolate on to the ice and top with a spoonful of cream.

Raspberry Delight

Illustrated opposite
Serves 4–6

Metric		Imperial
50 g	**castor sugar**	2 oz
few drops	**yellow food colouring**	few drops
1	**egg white, lightly beaten**	1
1 (40-g) packet	***Kellogg's Two Shakes* Raspberry Flavour**	1 (1.4-oz) packet
175 g	**unsweetened apple purée**	6 oz
15 ml	**lemon curd**	1 tablespoon
568 ml	**cold milk**	1 pint

Colour the castor sugar with a few drops of yellow colouring. Coat the rims of the glasses with a little egg white, then dip into the coloured sugar. Place the Raspberry *Two Shakes*, apple purée, lemon curd and milk into a blender for 30 seconds. Carefully pour into the frosted glasses and serve at once.

Raspberry Marshmallow Floats

Illustrated opposite
Serves 4–6

Metric		Imperial
1 (40-g) packet	***Kellogg's Two Shakes* Raspberry Flavour**	1 (1.4-oz) packet
5 ml	**ground cinnamon**	1 teaspoon
1 (128-g) packet	**marshmallows**	1 (4½-oz) packet
568 ml	**milk**	1 pint

Stir the Raspberry *Two Shakes*, cinnamon and most of the marshmallows with the milk in a saucepan. Heat slowly until the marshmallows dissolve. Pour into mugs or glasses and float the remaining marshmallows on top.

Chocolate icebreaker, Banana foam (see page 137), Raspberry marshmallow float (see above), Caribbean combo (see page 136), Raspberry delight (see above).

Kellogg's Product Index

Index

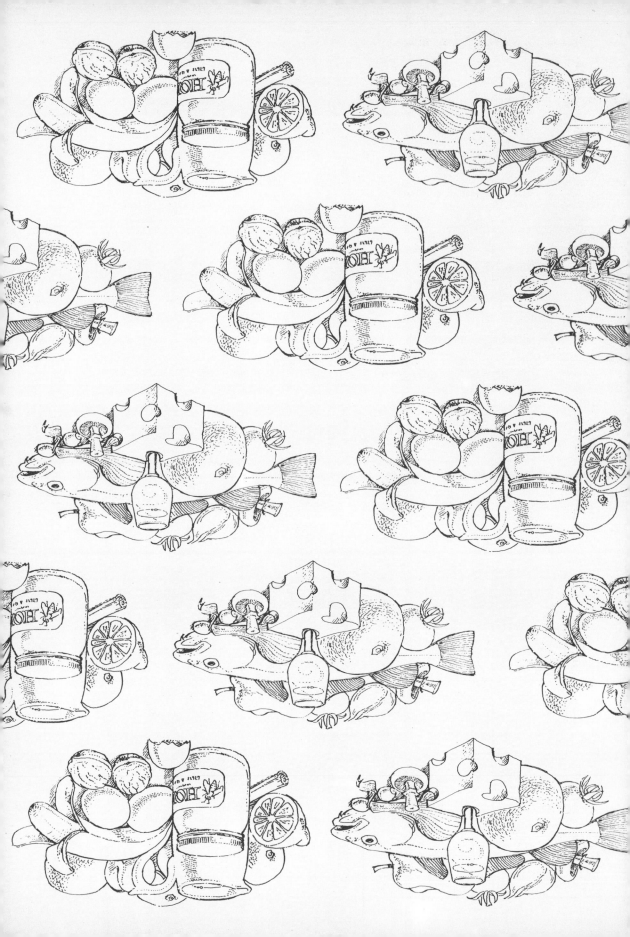